Praise for
24 Essential Lessons for Investment Success

"When it comes to investment and stock selection, you couldn't get a better mentor than Bill O'Neil. . . . A must read for the serious do-it-yourself investor."

HARRY S. DENT, JR.
Author
The Roaring 2000s and *The Roaring 2000s Investor*

"There simply isn't any other book that can be called a handbook for Cramer, Berkowitz."

JIM CRAMER
Co-founder, TheStreet.Com & Hedge Fund Manager
Cramer, Berkowitz & Co.

24 Essential Lessons for Investment Success

24 Essential Lessons for Investment Success

William J. O'Neil

McGraw-Hill

New York San Francisco Washington, D.C. Auckland Bogotá
Caracas Lisbon London Madrid Mexico City Milan
Montreal New Delhi San Juan Singapore
Sydney Tokyo Toronto

McGraw-Hill

A Division of The McGraw-Hill Companies

Copyright © 2000 by William J. O'Neil. All rights reserved. Printed in the United States of America. Except as permitted under the United States Copyright Act of 1976, no part of this publication may be reproduced or distributed in any form or by any means, or stored in a data base or retrieval system, without the prior written permission of the publisher.

  2 3 4 5 6 7 8 9 0 AGM/AGM 9 0 8 7 6 5 4 3 2 1 0 9 (IBD Edition)
1 2 3 4 5 6 7 8 9 0 AGM/AGM 9 0 8 7 6 5 4 3 2 1 0 9

ISBN 0-07-136033-6 (IBD Edition)
ISBN 0-07-135754-8

The editing supervisor was Janice Race, and the production supervisor was Elizabeth J. Strange. It was set in Minion by Jay's Publishers Services, Inc.

Printed and bound by Quebecor/Martinsburg.

McGraw-Hill books are available at special quantity discounts to use as premiums and sales promotions, or for use in corporate training programs. For more information, please write to the Director of Special Sales, McGraw-Hill, 11 West 19th Street, New York, NY 10011. Or contact your local bookstore.

 This book is printed on recycled, acid-free paper containing a minimum of 50% recycled, de-inked fiber.

Contents

Preface

These can truly be called the golden years for investors. Rarely have bull markets lasted so long or climbed so high. Yet millions of people remain on the sidelines, watching as a parade to increased wealth and financial security passes them by.

It's a shame. Most of us know social security will not meet our retirement needs. More than ever before, additional sources of income are necessary to maintain a comfortable standard of living. Beyond that, there is the real potential for financial freedom and security. So why aren't more people taking advantage of the tremendous investment opportunities in this country?

Lack of information is no longer a viable excuse. With the internet, individual investors have *more* access to *more* information than ever before. But therein lies a new challenge: separating the relevant information from the countless opinions, personal biases and promotions out there.

What's different about these 24 lessons is that they are based on a comprehensive study and analysis of the past 45 years of the stock market. This study discovered the principles and guidelines for how the market *actually* works, principles that have proven to work time and time again, regardless of market conditions and popular opinions.

We built models of the greatest stock market winners for every year going back to 1953—stocks that doubled, tripled, or even went up ten or twenty times in price. We analyzed, and continue to analyze, every bit of information known about these stocks to see what these big winners had in common *before* they made their biggest price moves. This research turned up seven common characteristics, some which will surprise you, that have remained constant year after year, cycle after cycle. That said, some of what you will read and come to learn will not necessarily be consistent with what you've heard before or believed to be true.

The chapters of this book will walk you through these seven characteristics. In addition, you will learn exactly how and when to buy and sell stocks, how to read charts, and how to use *Investor's Business Daily* to generate investment ideas and manage your portfolio.

In my experience, fear and uncertainty are the great inhibitors to success of any kind. If you haven't started investing yet, my hope for you is that this book will give you a solid foundation of knowledge and the courage to "get your feet wet." And if you're a seasoned investor, this book will help you achieve better results. It should also lend insights why you may have missed certain big winners in the past or perhaps failed to nail down some big profits when you had them.

Here's to your continued learning and even greater success!

Best regards,

William J. O'Neil

Acknowledgments

No book finds its way into the hands of readers without the teamwork and dedication of many hardworking individuals. In particular, I am grateful to Leila Marsden Barth, Heather Davis, Chris Gessel, Hilary Kircher and Jewell Maddox for their important contributions to this book as well as their unique and considerable talents. My heartfelt thanks go out to them.

LESSON 1

What Every Investor Should Know Going In

Before founding Investor's Business Daily *in 1984, Bill O'Neil already had 25 years of experience in the market as an individual investor, stock broker, investment adviser, and owner of a securities brokerage and research firm that today counts nearly every major institutional investor as a client. His career started at age 22, just after he graduated from Southern Methodist University, got married, joined the Air Force and became interested in his financial future. He bought his first stock with $500—all he had at the time. He also started reading books on the market. According to Bill O'Neil, the best was Gerald Loeb's* Battle for Investment Survival. *It's there we pick up our conversation.*

What is the single most important thing an investor should know?

Loeb was a highly successful investor and preached cutting all your losses short. And for me, this is rule #1. You must always protect your investment account. Particularly if you invest on margin (use borrowed money), cutting losses is absolutely essential.

Whether you're a new or experienced investor, the hardest lesson to learn is that you're simply not going to be right all the time. And if you don't cut every loss quickly, sooner or later you'll suffer some very large losses. I've known seven highly intelligent, educated men in their 40s who were wiped out because they invested on margin and had no sell discipline. Brains, education, ego, stubbornness and pride are deadly substitutes for having and following sound selling rules.

The problem is, you always hope to make money when you buy a stock. And when you have to sell and take a loss, you find it gut-wrenching and hard to admit you were wrong. You'd rather wait and hope the price will come back.

To make matters worse, when you do try to cut losses, half the time the stock will turn around and go back up in price. Then you're really upset. You conclude you were wrong for selling and that the loss-cutting policy is a bad one.

How you think about losses is critical. Historically, this is where most investors go wrong and get confused.

Ask yourself the following: Did you buy fire insurance on your house last year? Did your house burn down? If it didn't, were you upset because you wasted your money on the insurance? Will you refuse to buy fire insurance next year? Why do you buy fire insurance in the first place, because you know your home is going to burn down?

No! You buy insurance to protect yourself against the remote possibility you could suffer a major loss that would be difficult to recover from. That's all you do when you cut short your losses.

How do you define short?

For Loeb, it was 10%, which is probably a good rule for most beginning investors. But when you use charts to time your purchases more accurately, I recommend cutting all losses at 7% or 8% below your purchase price. By doing this, you're taking out little insurance policies to protect yourself from possible substantial losses.

If you let a stock go down 50% from where you bought it, you must make 100% on the next stock just to break even. Now, how often do you buy stocks that double in price?

How long did it take you to become successful investing?

It took me two to three years to figure out how to put the whole system together. It doesn't happen overnight. For most people the learning curve is about the same. As the years go by, you should get better and better at stock selection, and the number of individual 7% or 8% losses should drop significantly. Plus, these small losses will be offset by much larger profits from your big winners.

Think of a number of controlled losses as your tuition to Wall Street. Most people think that investing in a college degree is a sound decision. They don't think of it as a waste of money because they have hopes of having that degree pay off in future success. Why should success in the stock market be any different?

Anything worth succeeding at takes time to learn. Professional ballplayers aren't made in three months and neither are successful investors. The only difference between the successful person and everyone else is determination and persistence.

How persistent have you had to be at times?

I once had a string of ten stocks that I cut losses on. But the very next one emerged just as the market came out of a correction (downtrend) and more than tripled in price. I've often thought: "What would have happened if I had gotten discouraged and quit because the previous ten stocks I bought didn't work?"

The tricky part is getting rid of the emotion attached to making decisions, like cutting losses. It doesn't feel comfortable to sell something you may have purchased only a few weeks ago because it's now down 8% below your cost. Emotions take over. We try to defend our original decision to buy and justify holding the stock even though we're now in the negative.

But you can't go through life looking in the rear-view mirror. You can get yourself in a lot of trouble with the "could'ves," "would'ves" and "should'ves."

When you bought the stock, that was last week or last month—not today. Today is a whole different situation, and you've got to protect yourself from serious losses—which could happen to anyone—so you can still invest tomorrow.

Why did you pick 8% as the rule?

If you cut your losses at 8%, it will always allow you to survive to invest another day. I've seen people go bankrupt or ruin their health because they'd fall in love with a stock, couldn't face up to and admit mistakes, and couldn't make the hard sell decisions. Vacillating when it comes time to sell is how you will sooner or later experience big losses. And big losses will cause you to lose your confidence, which you absolutely cannot let happen if you expect to continue investing.

If you're worried, the old adage, "sell down to the sleeping point," is the best way to relieve some pressure. You don't have to sell it all, just sell something so you can sleep at night.

If you cut all your losses at 7% or 8% below your purchase price, and then sell just a few of your stocks when you're up 25% to 30%, you can be right once and wrong twice and still not get into trouble.

Your best-performing stocks should be held longer for a larger possible profit. Always sell your worst-performing stock first, not your best-performing stock.

What is the risk in any stock?

Under the method that I've laid out, your risk in any one stock is always limited to 8%, whether you're buying AT&T or the leading internet stock. So why not pick only the very best market leaders, companies in the leading industry groups that are #1 in their respective fields, and have strong return on equity, profit margins, and sales and earnings growth?

SUMMARY

- As a new investor, be prepared to take some small losses.
- Always cut your losses at 8% below your purchase price.
- Persistence is key when learning to invest. Don't get discouraged.
- Learning to invest doesn't happen overnight. It takes time and effort to become successful at it.

LESSON 2

Getting Started: There's No Time Like the Present!

In this lesson, Bill O'Neil discusses the first steps to investing, such as finding a broker, how much money it takes, and what types of investments you should focus on if you're just getting started.

Are some times better than others to start investing?

Any time is the right time. It takes most people a couple of years to really understand and learn to invest successfully. So it's important to get started in order to get the learning curve underway. You shouldn't wait until you get the perfect job or reach a certain age. You'll find that, with a bit of courage, preparation and determination, it can be well worth it.

What do you do first?

You open an account with a brokerage firm. It's very simple—much like opening an account at a bank. It boils down to filling out a few forms. Don't be afraid to ask questions.

First, decide whether you'll go with a full-service broker or a discount firm. If you're a new investor, a full-service brokerage might help in your education, since you'll have a broker who may be able to answer your questions.

It's important to know, however, that not all brokers do well in the market, so selecting a good one is critical. I'd suggest that you speak to the office manager. Explain you are interested in opening an account but want to focus on brokers who have made money in their own accounts as well as for the majority of their clients.

Find out something about the stock broker you're considering: what books they've read, what services they follow, where they get their information and what their general investment philosophy is. It is important to know that their data sources are of high quality. Do they subscribe to *Investor's Business Daily*? Also, are the brokers promoting their firm's new products, or are they truly interested in what products are right for you? You want to make sure you are getting the best representation you can.

If you opt for a discount brokerage, I would not seek out the one with the absolute lowest commissions (the amount a firm charges per trade). You want service and quality from a firm that's likely to stay in business for many years.

Are there different types of accounts?

I'd suggest opening a cash account at first and then, after a few years of experience, consider a margin account that lets you borrow money from your broker.

Then what?

Plan to spend at least several hours each week keeping track of your investments and the market. Also, be very careful when listening to other people and their advice. Most of it will be nothing more than personal opinion and is probably faulty.

You should subscribe to a chart service and learn to read charts. They merely lay out facts for you, not opinions. (Lessons 9, 10, and 11 cover how to read charts.)

What types of investments should be avoided?

Being a new investor, you should avoid the most speculative areas, such as low-priced stocks, futures, options, and foreign stocks because of their risk and volatility.

With low-priced stocks, you get what you pay for. I would rather buy 50 shares of a $60 stock than 300 shares of a $10 stock. Institutional investors will put millions of dollars into the $60 stock, and most will shun low-priced issues. And, as we'll discuss later on, it's the large institutions—the mutual funds, pension funds and banks—that do most of the trading in the market and really make stocks move in price.

You're investing dollars. The number of shares you buy is irrelevant. You want to invest your dollars in the best companies, not the cheapest. Most of the outstanding companies you select to invest in should be between $15 and $150 a share.

How much money does it take to get started?

It takes only $500 to $1,000 to get started, and you can add to your investment account from savings from your salary. The important things are to get started and gain experience.

Running a paper portfolio isn't the same thing as having your money on the line in the real battlefield of the market.

There's an old trader's story about a man who was going to duel. He bragged that he was an expert marksman with a pistol and could crack the stem of a wine glass at 100 yards. His companion remarked, "Yes, but can you do it with a loaded pistol pointed at your heart?"

Paper trading simply doesn't let you experience the hope, fear, excitement and greed that are injected into investment decisions when you're under real pressure with your hard-earned money on the line.

How many stocks should someone own?

If you have $5,000 or less, you should own no more than two stocks. If you have $10,000, two or three stocks is appropriate. With $25,000, perhaps three or four; with $50,000, four or five; and with $100,000 or more, you should own five or six.

There's no reason to own twenty or more stocks. You simply can't know all you need to know about that many. You'll also dilute your overall results.

For the individual investor, real money is made first by buying stocks of the very best companies in their fields, and then by concentrating your portfolio on a limited number and watching them carefully. I don't believe in the principle of wide diversification, or trying to reduce risk by spreading your money across many stocks or many types of investments (asset allocation will be discussed in Lesson 19).

What investing books are worthwhile?

If you're new to the market, the *Investor's Business Daily Guide to the Markets* is a great primer. I personally have a library of more than 2,000 books on the market, but only a few are really outstanding.

Some that I read early on that helped me are: Gerald Loeb's *Battle for Investment Survival*, Edwin Lefevre's *Reminiscences of a Stock Operator* and Bernard Baruch's autobiography, *My Own Story*.

I have summed up much of what I've learned over the years in my own book, *How to Make Money in Stocks*.

SUMMARY

- When getting started, it is important that you pick the right full-service or discount brokerage. If you use a broker, make sure he or she has a good track record.
- As a beginner, set up a cash account, not a margin account.
- It only takes $500 to $1,000 to get started. Experience is a great teacher.
- Avoid more volatile types of investments, such as futures, options and foreign stocks.
- Concentrate on a few, high-quality stocks. There's no need to own twenty or more stocks.

LESSON 3

Follow a System Rather Than Your Emotions

Jesse Livermore, a famous old trader, who made and lost millions in the stock market, once said: "There are only two emotions in the market—hope and fear. The problem is, you hope when you should fear, and you fear when you should hope." In this lesson, Bill O'Neil provides insights on how to keep emotions out of investment decisions.

What did Livermore mean by "hoping" when you should "fear" and vice versa?

When a stock falls 8% below your cost and you're losing money, you hope it'll go back up. But you really should be fearing that you might lose more money. And you should react by selling the stock and cutting the loss.

When a stock goes up in price and you're making money, you fear you might lose your profit. So you sell too soon. But the fact that the stock is going up is actually a sign of strength and an indication that you may be right.

Isn't that against human nature?

Whenever your own money is on the line, it's going to be emotional, and the stock market is no exception. But the market doesn't know who you are. And frankly, it doesn't care what you think or what you would like to see happen.

Human nature is deeply embedded in the market, and the same emotions of ego, gullibility, fear and greed that existed yesterday continue today.

How do you overcome these natural, yet potentially costly, emotional reactions?

In my experience, the only way is to establish buying and selling rules derived from historical research—rules based on how the market *actually* works, not on personal opinions and preconceived ideas.

Lawyers analyze history and use precedents, so why shouldn't you? The more you know about the past, the more you'll be able to recognize future opportunities.

How is the past helpful in the case of the stock market?

We've built models, or profiles, of every outstanding stock each year beginning in 1953. Rather than listening to supposed experts, personal opinions, hot tips and rumors, many of which are faulty, I know exact-ly what the characteristics of the biggest winners of the past were—a recipe for successful stocks that can guide me as I seek tomorrow's new leaders.

Analyzing history also provides perspective on the market as a whole. Daily and weekly market fluctuations intimidate even the most experienced investors. But a look at the past will show that there's an overall uptrend in the market, cycle after cycle, that creates a huge ongo-ing opportunity for investors.

So knowing the facts and examining history are the keys?

They're important. But so are developing sound habits and sticking to the rules. And that's the harder part. It can be even more difficult for individuals who have followed unhealthy investing habits for years and years. Changing these frailties is a real challenge and takes consid-erable effort.

What are some of the worst habits investors have?

One is an overwhelming attraction to low-priced stocks. The idea of buying a large block of a $2, $5 or $10 stock and watching it double sounds wonderful. The only problem: your odds of winning the lottery may be better.

The fact is, investing in stocks is not the same thing as buying a dress or a car on sale. The market is an auction marketplace: Stocks sell for what they're worth at the time. And when you buy cheap stocks, you get what you pay for.

Of the best-performing stocks of the last 45 years, the average per-share price before they went on to double or triple or more was $28 a share. This is a historical fact. Cheap stocks involve far greater risk.

So should that be the minimum?

I do not buy stocks under $15 a share. Of my really huge winners over the years, I bought them between $16 and $100 a share.

15

Sound scary? Don't laugh: the $100 stock went to the equivalent of $550 a share. The outstanding companies that are leaders in their fields just simply do not come off the launching pad at $5 or $10. There are very few, if any, exceptions to this rule.

Many people want to get rich overnight, which just does not happen. Success takes time and a willingness to objectively and honestly analyze your mistakes. That's the key to getting smarter at anything in life.

Admitting mistakes isn't easy, is it?

No one likes to be wrong. But letting your ego get in the way of proper analysis of a prior action, or falling in love with a stock and failing to look at it objectively, are simply not sound when it comes to the market.

An invaluable tool I've found is to do a post-analysis of all my trades. Every year, I jot down the point on a daily chart where I bought and sold every stock, as well as the reasons I bought or sold each one.

Then I separate those I made money on from those where I lost money. What was I doing right on the stocks that went up? What mistakes did I make with the others?

I then make a few new rules that will prevent the same mistakes in the future. If you don't look at what you're doing wrong, you'll never become a better investor.

SUMMARY

- Don't get emotionally involved with your stocks. Follow a set of buying and selling rules, and don't let your emotions change your mind.
- Don't buy a stock under $15 a share. The best companies that are the leaders in their fields simply do not come at $5 or $10 per share.
- Learning from the best stock market winners can guide you to tomorrow's leaders.
- Always do a post-analysis of your stock market trades so that you can learn from your successes and mistakes.

LESSON 4

Fundamental Analysis or Technical Analysis?

Methods of analyzing a stock for potential investment generally fall into two camps: fundamental or technical. And investors are constantly debating which is better. In this lesson, Bill O'Neil discusses why both methods are essential to investment success.

Where do you come down in the fundamental vs. the technical debate?

From my experience, it's definitely not an "either-or" question. Rather than limiting yourself, you must consider *both* fundamental information about the strength, quality, and soundness of the company and its products and the technical side of how a stock is performing in the marketplace.

Fundamental analysis is the foundation you must have behind every stock you buy. This will determine the quality and superiority of the stock. It's how you separate the wheat from the chaff.

What's most important in fundamental analysis?

We've found that a company's profitability is one of the most important factors that affect the stock price. This means buying *only* stocks that show consistent earnings improvement, have increased sales and have preferably both strong profit margins and a high return on equity.

Earnings per share (calculated by dividing a company's total after-tax profits by the number of common shares outstanding) can be used as an indicator of growth and profitability.

From our study of the most successful stocks in the past, coupled with years of experience, we found that three out of four of the biggest winners were growth stocks, companies with annual earnings per share growth rates up an average of 30% or more—for each of the past three years—before they made their biggest price gains. Therefore, concentrate on stocks with annual earnings growth rates of 30% or more for the past three years.

In my own stock selection, this is one of the most significant rules.

What if a company doesn't have three years of earnings history?

Some initial public offerings, and companies that went public in the last eight or ten years, may not have three years of earnings growth. There is a tendency to think that IPOs do not have three years of earnings, but in most cases they do have earnings data from when they were privately held. This information can be found in company prospectuses. In these special cases, I want to see earnings in each of the last six quarters up a material amount (50% or more) compared to the same quarter the year before.

I'm not interested in promises that losses or mediocre earnings will improve in the future. The vast majority of our successful historical models all had strong, accelerating earnings *before* their huge price increases began.

What other fundamental factors are vital?

Sales should either be accelerating in the last few quarters or be up 25% or more from the same quarter one year earlier. I also prefer to select companies that are #1 in their particular fields in terms of recent sales and earnings growth, profit margins and return on equity.

What is "return on equity"?

Return on equity (ROE), is an indicator of financial performance. It measures how efficient a company is with its money.

Most of the big winners in our study had ROEs of 20% or more. Many were recent new issues (IPOs). Most also had management ownership. That is, management owned a certain percentage of the outstanding stock, giving them a higher stake in the company's future performance.

Anything else on the fundamental side?

The company should have a unique or exceptional new product or service that is perceived to be superior. You should understand what the company you're investing in makes or does.

The stock should also have strong institutional sponsorship and in most cases be in a leading industry group. Knowing how many of the better-performing mutual funds, banks and other institutional investors have bought a stock can serve as your personal research department. The top institutions usually do thorough fundamental analysis before they buy large stock positions.

How is technical analysis different from fundamental?

Technical analysis is the study of market movement, mainly with the use of charts. Chart analysis uses a stock's price and volume movements as the leading indicators and allows you to check out the supply and demand for a stock.

You should use daily or weekly price charts with trading volume data. By using charts, you can graphically see if a stock is acting normal or abnormal, if it's under accumulation (professional buying) or not, and if it's the right time to buy or sell, based on its own history.

Part of this system is learning to identify sound price patterns, or bases, to help you determine possible future price movement (refer to Chapters 9, 10, and 11 in *How to Make Money in Stocks* for more information on base patterns).

Why do you use both fundamental and technical analysis?

Because a price and volume chart may alert me to a potential problem or opportunity earlier than changes in fundamental numbers.

Volume, or the number of shares a stock trades per day or per week, is one of your big keys to interpreting supply and demand correctly. It's important to know if your stock is going up or down in price on greater- or less-than-normal volume. This is why we provide the "Volume Percent Change" column in *Investor's Business Daily*'s stock tables.

Volume is a signal that big institutions may be buying or selling your stock, which could impact the price either positively or negatively. Some time in the future, this critical data might save your neck.

The best institutional investors use both fundamental and technical analysis in their purchase decisions.

SUMMARY

- A combination of fundamental and technical investment styles is essential to picking winning stocks.
- Fundamental analysis looks at a company's earnings, earnings growth, sales, profit margins, and return on equity among other things. It helps narrow down your choices so that you are only dealing with quality stocks.
- Technical analysis involves learning to read a stock's price and volume chart and timing your decisions properly.

LESSON 5

First Among Fundamentals: Earnings and Sales

In Bill O'Neil's "45-Year Study of the Greatest Stock Market Winners," he discovered that earnings and sales growth were two of the most important fundamental factors. In this lesson, Bill O'Neil gives real-life examples of companies that demonstrate these winning characteristics.

What's the main thing that separates the really successful investors from those who only get average results?

Your objective is not to be right all the time. It's to make big money when you are right and to get out early when you appear to be wrong. To make big money, you've got to buy the very best. Companies that are #1 in their fields are the real market leaders.

How do you find the big winners?

We've found that strong sales and earnings were among the most important characteristics of winning stocks. This becomes obvious when you see what really great companies looked like in terms of their sales, earnings and profit margins *before* they launched price increases of 200% to 1,000% or more.

You're looking for strong increases in quarterly sales and earnings compared to the same quarter the year before. You also want to see acceleration in the percent increases in quarterly earnings over the most recent quarters.

What are some examples?

In October 1986, six months after its initial public offering, Microsoft's latest-quarter sales were up 68%, and its earnings were up 75%. This quarterly earnings gain was its seventh in a row.

In March 1982, six months after its IPO, Home Depot's earnings were up 140% in the most recent quarter. Sales in the most recent three quarters accelerated from +104% to +158% to +191%, with the last nine quarters each averaging +177%.

In 1990, Cisco Systems' earnings were up in the prior nine quarters from +150% to +1,100%, with the average being +443%.

When I purchased Price Co. in April 1981, it showed fourteen quarters of large sales and earnings increases.

This is what I mean when I refer to the fundamental sales and earning power behind the biggest winners. All of these stocks had enormous gains *after* posting these sales and earnings figures.

Any other fundamentals to look for besides quarterly sales and earnings?

You should also look for growth in annual earnings—a longer-term indicator.

Microsoft's annual earnings growth rate was 99% at the point it took off in 1986, and Cisco Systems' was 57% in 1990. Price Co.'s annual earnings growth rate showed 90%.

These leaders also displayed a strong return on equity and healthy pre-tax profit margins. The ROEs of Microsoft, Home Depot and Cisco Systems were 40%, 28% and 36%, respectively, and Microsoft and Cisco Systems both had pre-tax profit margins of 33%.

All of this happened *before* they went on to make their biggest price increases during the 1990s. My rule of thumb is: Look for stocks with annual earnings growth rates of 30% or more and ROEs of 17% or higher.

Where do you find these measurements?

Years ago, our research and brokerage firm developed a database driven, proprietary rating system that would benefit our institutional clients when evaluating current and longer-term earnings performance.

The Earnings Per Share (EPS) Rating, available to individual investors every day *only* in *Investor's Business Daily*'s stock tables, combines each company's two most recent quarters earnings per share growth with its three- to five-year annual growth rate. It then compares each company with every other publicly traded company in order to provide a relative earnings rating.

On a scale from 1 to 99, a company with a 99 EPS Rating is in the top 1% of all companies in terms of its earnings growth record.

Consider this: Both Microsoft and Cisco Systems had EPS Ratings of 99 *prior* to their huge gains.

Just how big were those gains?

Microsoft was up 266% in only thirty weeks from the period in 1986, Home Depot was up 912% in less than 1 1/2 years from 1982, and Cisco Systems and Price Co. advanced 2,000% and 750%, respectively, since 1990 and 1982.

Anything else to look for?

My last suggestion is the most important. If you come to understand and have the courage to implement it, you could find the next Microsoft and make a fortune.

The major price advances of all the stocks I've mentioned followed periods of price correction and base-building in which the prices made no real progress.

These chart bases were almost always formed specifically because of a decline or correction in the general market averages. In each case, when the market finally turned, had a clear "follow-through," and began a new uptrend, these leaders were the first stocks in the market to advance into new-high ground.

In October 1990, as soon as the general market turned, Cisco Systems was one of the first out of the gate with a gain of $7, from $22 to $29 in one week alone, indicating its early leadership.

Sounds as if you look at bear markets or corrections in a different way from most people.

I think of them as huge opportunities, because all the future big leaders are building bases and will rebound fast, whether it's tomorrow or three months later when the general market finally snaps out of its correction. It's a period you absolutely never want to miss.

SUMMARY

- To make big money, you have got to buy the very best companies at the right time.

- Strong sales and earnings are among the most important characteristics of winning stocks.
- Look for stocks with strong and continuous increases in quarterly earnings. You also want annual earnings growth of 30% or more. The EPS Rating combines these for you and shows you how your stock is doing compared to all other stocks.
- Look for ROEs of 17% or higher.
- Buying a stock as it is coming out of a price consolidation area or base is crucial to making large gains.

LESSON 6

Relative Price Strength: A Key Technical Tool

Relative price strength can be a confusing, yet very useful indicator for investors. In this lesson, Bill O'Neil explains relative price strength in detail, showing how to use it and clearing up the misconceptions many investors have.

Why do you place so much emphasis on how a stock is performing compared to all other companies? When searching for superior companies, why not only look at outstanding sales and earnings?

Relative price strength is one key technical indicator that shows you what value the market itself places upon a stock. How is a stock's price acting in relation to the market and all other stocks? We calculate the Relative Price Strength Rating by taking a stock's price one year ago and its price today, calculating the percent change and then comparing it to all other stocks over the same time period. Like Earnings Per Share Rating, the results are placed on a simple scale of 1 to 99, with 99 being the highest.

In our studies of all outstanding stocks since 1953, the average Relative Price Strength Rating of these superperformers at the beginning of their huge increases of several hundred to several thousand percent was 87. That means these stocks outperformed 87% of all other stocks in the prior year. Only *Investor's Business Daily*'s stock tables give you an updated Relative Price Strength Rating for each stock every business day.

How do you use relative price strength to pick stocks?

I suggest you restrict your stock selection to stocks showing a Relative Price Strength Rating of 80 or higher, so you're selecting companies that are in the top 20% in performance. The true leaders will probably show a Relative Price Strength Rating of 85 or higher. Relative Price Strength Rating helps you cut out the vast number of laggard, mediocre performing companies that will hold back your overall performance.

I never argue with the market by trying to buy or hold stocks with a poor Relative Price Strength Rating of 70 or below.

In addition to using the Relative Price Strength Rating, you should get used to checking a stock's relative price strength line (available in most chart services), shown below each stock's price history (the price line).

When you're trying to choose which two or three stocks to buy, I would tend toward the one showing the best angle up in the relative price strength line on a chart. You never want to buy stocks with the relative price strength line in a general decline over the past six to twelve months. I'll go into detail on how to read charts in Lessons 9, 10, and 11.

As with people, you can tell a lot about a stock by the company it keeps. There should be at least one other stock in the same industry group that is showing strong price action (a high Relative Price Strength Rating) as well. *Investor's Business Daily* also provides an Industry Group Relative Strength Rating that will give you an idea of how a stock's group fares against 196 other industries based on the group's price action. If you can't find any other strong stocks in the group or, as a group, an industry is underperforming, perhaps you may want to rethink your selection. It usually pays to buy in a leading industry group.

Can a stock's Relative Price Strength Rating help you make your sell decisions?

Relative price performance is a good way to tell which of the five or six stocks you own is your true leader. Monthly or quarterly, rank your stocks based on their percentage price change for that time period. If you're going to do any selling, it's normally correct to weed the flower patch by selling your worst-performing stocks first. I also like to note on big down days in the general market which individual stocks buck the trend and are actually up in price an unusual amount for the day.

What if a stock with a strong Relative Price Strength Rating falls right after you buy it? Shouldn't you stick with the leaders?

If the stock you buy goes down in price, don't buy more. As stated in the first lesson of this book, you should sell any stock that falls 8% below the price you paid for it in order to protect yourself. That was rule #1. Averaging down (buying more as the stock drops in price) is dangerous. You may get away with it sometimes, but in the long run, it's always a risky proposition for individual investors to put good money after bad.

If you buy a stock on the way down at $50 a share and then buy more at $45, what do you do when the stock goes to $40 and then $35? What if the stock doesn't come back? It's much wiser to carefully average up in price, as a stock moves up. This is where you want to put your money, not in stocks with lagging price action.

If a stock has been holding an RS Rating in the 80s or 90s for many months, the first time its rating drops below 70 may be a good time to re-evaluate your position and consider selling.

SUMMARY

- Relative price strength is one key technical indicator that shows you what value the market itself places upon a stock.

- When using IBD *SmartSelect*™ Corporate Ratings, avoid stocks that have a Relative Price Strength Rating below 80. Always go with strength when picking stocks.

- If a stock's relative strength falls, do not buy any more shares. If the stock price drops 8% below your purchase price, sell *all* of your shares. This way you can protect yourself from large losses.

LESSON 7

Know a Stock by the Company It Keeps

Like people, stocks tend to move in groups. In this lesson, Bill O'Neil explains the importance of industry groups and sectors, and how you can tell which industry groups are leading the market.

Why is it important for you to learn to select stocks that are in a leading industry or sector?

First of all, sectors are much broader than industry groups. The consumer sector, for example, comprises a number of broad-reaching industries including retail, automobiles and household appliances. Since 1953, the majority of individual stocks that were the real market leaders were also part of a leading industry group or sector at the time.

For example, in recent years when Microsoft was an outstanding winner, so was PeopleSoft (computer software); when Dell was outperforming, so was Compaq (computer hardware); when Home Depot began outperforming in the second quarter of 1997, so did Wal-Mart and The Gap, all three of which are in the retail group. About that same time, Schering-Plough and Bristol-Myers Squibb surged into leadership, and so did Warner Lambert and Pfizer, all from the pharmaceutical area. It's clear that stocks tend to move in groups or sectors. When I buy a stock, I always like to see at least one other stock in the same group that is also showing strength.

In addition to specific industry groups that are strongest at a particular time, there is another crucial type of sector move that you should learn to spot: Are big institutions primarily investing in the larger, blue-chip growth stocks or the more volatile, less seasoned small-cap companies?

Late in 1997, the market shifted its emphasis from smaller companies to highly liquid big-capitalization stocks. With larger numbers of shares of stock available in big-cap, better established stocks, money managers can get in or out of a stock more easily. It pays to be alert and invest where the big money is flowing. You can tell when the market shifts from small-caps to big-caps by tracking the small chart entitled "Big-Cap Growth Funds vs. Small-Cap Growth Funds," published daily on *Investor's Business Daily*'s "Industry Groups" page.

How do you spot such changes in leadership?

Here's what you can do. Once you've found a stock that fits all of the fundamental measurements of consistent sales and earnings growth and strong profitability, and the timing is right on the technical side (which

I'll show you how to recognize), check the strength of its industry group. *Investor's Business Daily* has a list of 197 industry groups ranked by their group's relative price performance, using all stocks in each group for the last six months.

This table is comprehensive in that it doesn't just show you one computer industry, it shows you all of the specific subgroups of the industry. The software industry is broken into six subgroups—such as desktop, financial and medical. You gain a much more defined and focused perspective on a particular industry.

Why is this valuable?

Because you want to be in the best subgroup of an industry. Perhaps computer services are leading and computer graphics are lagging. The top 20% of the 197 industry groups are usually best, and I recommend avoiding the bottom 20%. *Investor's Business Daily*'s main stock tables include the stock's Industry Group Relative Strength Rating on an A to E scale with A being highest. A and B rated stocks are preferred. This detailed information can't be found in any other publication.

A second, and even better place to find the market's leading industry groups is *Investor's Business Daily*'s "52-Week Highs & Lows" feature ("New Highs" list).

It's organized by sectors with the most stocks making new price highs. When you're in a positive market with numerous stocks making new highs, the top five or six sectors on this list will be your leaders. I check out this list every single day so I'm always aware of what the top groups are and can spot when a brand new group shows up in the top part of this innovative list. Use of this list should increase most investors performance at least 10% to 20%.

The retail group popped up near the top of the list at the beginning of 1998 for the first time in several years. Any time you have thirty or forty stocks in a sector making new highs, that's a powerful clue you can't afford to ignore.

Another special list in *Investor's Business Daily* entitled "Groups with the Greatest % of Stocks Making New Highs" also provides valuable clues. It's in a somewhat smaller box located below the"52-Week Highs & Lows" feature ("New Highs" list) on the "Industry Groups" page.

Historically, the drugs and medical, computer, communications technology, software, specialty retail, and leisure and entertainment groups have supplied more big winners than most other groups. It's also of value to consider the big picture. We won the Cold War. The U.S. is basically a giant consumer nation, and we are leaders in the information, high-tech, and brave new internet worlds. Our baby boomer population is getting older, so now is a time when investing, leisure, and medicine become more important.

It's also critical to understand that automobiles, steel, aluminum, machinery, airlines, railroads, copper and building are cyclical industries that may make shorter runs when they begin moving up. Additionally, most high-tech industry stocks are twice as volatile as most consumer groups and so they have added risk as well as potential reward.

A third and fourth vital clue to market sector movement can be found on *Investor's Business Daily*'s "General Market & Sectors" page: sector charts, which are listed in order of their relative price strength, and a small box, "Market Sector Indexes." Both will give you a good feel for where the true sector leadership is.

A complete listing of industry groups and the stocks that make up each group is available separately from *Investor's Business Daily*. The *Industry Group and Ticker Symbol Index* is updated twice a year.

SUMMARY

- Always pick stocks from the leading industry groups or sectors. The majority of past market leaders were in the top industry groups and sectors.

- Many big winning stocks come from sectors such as drugs and medical, computers, communications technology, software, specialty retail, and leisure and entertainment.

- The Industry Group Relative Strength Rating can help you identify stocks in the top industries.

The Importance of Volume and Sponsorship

The biggest players in the market are mutual funds and big institutions. In this lesson, Bill O'Neil discusses the impact these institutions have on the market and how individual investors can track what the institutions are trading.

What is volume and why is it important?

The law of supply and demand is rampant in the marketplace. Stocks never go up in price by accident—there must be large buying demand. Most of this demand comes from institutional investors, who account for more than 75% of buying of the better quality leading stocks. When you're selecting stocks, daily or weekly trading volume is how you measure demand.

Volume is the actual number of shares traded daily and is available in most daily newspapers. However, unless you're tracking this information day to day in order to recognize excessive volume (which may indicate large buying or selling), these publications are not very helpful.

Only *Investor's Business Daily* gives you "Volume Percent Change" for every stock, every day. This measurement, found in the stock tables, tracks the average daily volume of every stock over the past fifty trading days and shows you how much a stock traded yesterday above or below its average. For example, a stock showing a "+356" volume percentage change in *Investor's Business Daily*'s stock tables indicates that stock traded 356% more volume yesterday compared to its average daily volume over the last fifty days. Additionally, *Investor's Business Daily* provides special screened lists daily which identify stocks with the greatest percentage rise in volume. These valuable "Where the Big Money's Flowing" lists precede the NYSE and Nasdaq tables each day.

It's impossible for big institutions to buy a stock without it showing up in either *Investor's Business Daily*'s "Volume Percent Change" column in the stock tables or in the "Where the Big Money's Flowing" lists at the beginning of the NYSE and Nasdaq tables. To give you an idea of just how big this buying is, if a single fund has $1 billion in assets and wants just a 2% new position in a stock, they must invest $20 million. That's 500,000 shares of a stock selling at $40 per share! Funds are just like elephants jumping into a bathtub. They are simply so big the water rises and splashes all over the place. *Investor's Business Daily* enables you to easily track the institutional elephants.

O.K., the volume tells me a stock's being traded heavily. How do I know if it's being bought or sold?

Investor's Business Daily has another proprietary gauge that can be very helpful in identifying whether a stock is being bought or sold: the Accumulation/Distribution Rating. It is available for every stock, every day, and the Acc/Dist Rating tracks the last thirteen weeks of trading volume for a stock and tells you whether it is under accumulation (institutional buying) or distribution (institutional selling). Provided on an A to E rating system, an A or B means the stock is being bought, a D or E means it's being sold and should probably be avoided for the time being, and a C indicates a neutral amount of buying and selling.

What is sponsorship?

It's when large institutional investors buy into a stock. If you really want to buy stocks that could go up a significant amount, it is essential that the prospect you select has at least one or two better performing institutional investors that have bought a new position in the stock recently. My research shows that new buys taken in the last quarter are most important and large additions to existing positions are second in importance.

How can I find out who the better performers are and what they're buying and selling?

All you have to do is get in the habit of checking *Investor's Business Daily*'s Mutual Fund section. It contains informative reports on all of the top-performing funds over the last three years. Another proprietary rating, the 36 Month Performance Rating, compares every fund, regardless of type, and rates them on a grading scale. A fund with an A+ rating is in the top 5% of all funds. An A is in the top 10%, an A– in the top 15%, a B+ in the top 20% and so on. This is your key to identifying the best performing funds.

In this section, there are also special lists jam-packed with other key data about better performing funds, such as a fund's ten largest stock holdings by dollar amount, new stock purchases (indicated by an "N" beside the stock's name) and which stocks a fund has added to or reduced its positions in (indicated by a "+" or "–" beside the stock's name). Their top ten holdings generally are more relevant than other, smaller holdings.

Also shown are a fund's top ten new buys in the recently reported period in order of the largest dollar commitments. I am particularly interested in the top three or four new purchases. Where a top-performing fund placed its largest buys tells you where it had the most conviction. By checking daily, you will become aware when several different funds have taken a new position or have been selling a stock you may have an interest in.

For example, I checked *Investor's Business Daily*'s Mutual Fund section on August 24, 1998. It showed that as of June 30, MAS Funds Mid Cap Growth, whose *Investor's Business Daily* performance rating was A+, sold large amounts of Complete Business Solutions, Advanced Fibre Communications, Ciena, Franklin Resources, PeopleSoft and Dollar Tree. If you owned one of these stocks at the time, this could have been important information for you to know. You cannot find this type of valuable data in any other newspaper or on the internet.

But why are a fund's purchases from two months ago relevant today?

Most funds publicly report their holdings quarterly or semiannually about five or six weeks after the end of their particular period. Many people assume this is too late to be of value, which is not true.

How do you tell if it's too late to buy?

Always check a daily or weekly chart on the stocks mentioned as recent top fund buys. Are these stocks in a sound chart base or buying area (we'll show you how to recognize one in Lesson 9) or are they too far extended in price above their last proper base and therefore too risky to buy? There is a timing question, and we'll show you how to spot the best time to buy stocks recently purchased by top funds.

Others think they should buy a stock before any funds own it, hoping the funds will run it up in price after they discover the stock. This is shortsighted. There are thousands of institutional investors today, many with billions in resources. If none of the better performing funds has bought a particular stock, I would stay away. Ask yourself: Why did they steer clear? Whether right or wrong, it still takes their heavy buying to move a stock up consistently. So you want to buy stocks that have at least a few of the better mutual funds making recent new purchases.

By regularly following the *Investor's Business Daily* Mutual Fund section, you will learn something about the kind of stocks the best professionals buy and do not buy. They do not purchase cheap stocks, but rather, higher-quality companies that can accommodate their volume buying. You also can determine the industries they are putting the most money into as well as the areas where they are retreating. It is wise to note whether the total number of funds buying a stock has steadily increased over the last few quarters.

How can I tell if my stock is sponsored by institutional investors?

Investor's Business Daily has yet another proprietary gauge called Sponsorship Rating, published in the stock tables every Tuesday. Each stock's sponsorship is rated on an easy scale from A to E. An A or B rating means better performing funds own the stock and/or the number of funds owning the stock has been increasing in recent quarters.

SUMMARY

- Volume is the actual number of shares traded.
- Stocks never go up by accident. There must be large buying, typically from big investors such as mutual funds and pension funds.
- *Investor's Business Daily*'s "Volume Percent Change" column tracks the average daily volume of every stock over the past fifty trading days and shows you how much a stock traded above or below its average.

- Use Accumulation/Distribution Rating to find out if stocks are being bought or sold by big institutional investors.
- It's important to know what stocks the best mutual funds are buying and selling. Sponsorship Rating helps you determine whether your stock has quality institutional sponsorship.

LESSON 9

How to Buy at Just the Right Moment

When investigating a stock, it is important to look at a chart to see how it is performing technically. In this lesson, Bill O'Neil explains the basics of chart reading and introduces you to one key pattern: the "cup with handle."

As long as the fundamentals are solid, does it really matter when you buy a stock?

We've all heard the saying, "timing is everything." This is just as true in the stock market as it is in life. Knowing the optimal time to buy or sell a stock is a valuable skill anyone can and should learn. In the next three lessons, I'm going to show you how to read a stock's daily or weekly chart, which will give you a visual picture of how a stock's price and trading volume change over a period of time can lend clues to its future performance.

Charts are essential because they communicate critical information about how a stock is acting in the marketplace—information you would miss by concentrating on fundamentals alone. Charts are graphic depictions of historical price and trading volume behavior. They allow you to identify current behavior in relation to a stock's recent history.

On a chart's price line, each vertical bar represents a day's (or week's) price action in terms of three variables. The top of the bar represents the highest price the stock traded for that day (intra-day high price). The bottom of the bar marks the low price of the day (intra-day low price). The horizontal intersecting slash shows where the stock closed for that period. At the bottom of the chart is a graphic depiction of the volume that traded for that same period, daily or weekly.

But how do you make sense of all those bars and slashes?

We've discussed the importance of volume. Now let's make the connection between volume and price. A constructive sign easily identified on a chart is large increased volume from the day or week before with the price moving up. This normally indicates accumulation, or professional buying, of a stock. A sign of potential trouble, or distribution (professional selling), is increasing volume as a stock drops in price.

On the flip side, if the price is trending down, but the volume is also trending down significantly, there may be little cause for worry in that the decreased volume shows the stock is not being heavily sold. However, like most things, it's not quite this simple. In the next lesson, I will go over specific exceptions to these generalities. I use both technical and fundamental indicators because there may be signals that appear in a chart, on the technical side, that may precede publicly or professionally known changes in the fundamentals. This is especially true when leading stocks hit their price tops. Some stocks can top while current earnings and estimated earnings look great.

During our "45-Year Study of the Greatest Stock Market Winners," in addition to looking at fundamental measurements, we focused on the technical indicators of price and volume movements and patterns by studying charts on all the outstanding stocks. What we found in common was that price consolidation areas or specific types of base patterns occurred in the stock's price movement. These bases were formed just before the stocks broke out into new high ground in price and then went on to make their biggest gains. These base patterns were usually caused by corrections in the general market indices.

So what does the chart of a future big leader look like just before it's ready to break out to a new high in price and advance 100% to 200% or more?

There are three primary patterns. One of the most common we named a "cup with handle."

It was named this because the general shape resembles the outline of a coffee cup (see the graph on the next page). Points A to B is the left-hand declining part of the cup, B is the bottom rounding out process of the cup with the price going back and forth for a few weeks, and from B to C, the stock rallies back up in price to a point usually just below its old high. Then C to D to E forms the handle. The entire area from Point A to Point E is called a "cup with handle."

Also, as part of our study of these winners, I identified an optimal buy point, or "pivot point," for a stock. How? This point, usually at the end of a sound basing area when the stock price breaks out into new high ground, is the point of least resistance. This means that at this point, the stock has its greatest chance of moving even higher based on its current and historical price and volume activity.

In the "cup with handle" pattern shown, the correct time to buy the stock would be as soon as it trades one-eighth of a point above the peak

Reading The Pattern

Here's how a "cup with handle" base looks in theory and in practice

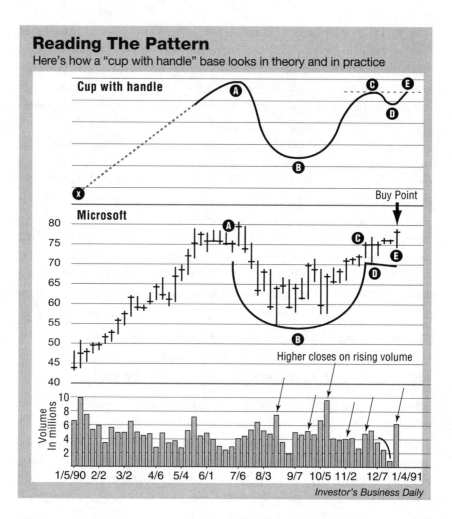

Cup with handle

A · B · C · D · E · X

Buy Point

Microsoft

80
75
70
65
60
55
50
45
40

Higher closes on rising volume

Volume
In millions
10
8
6
4
2

1/5/90 2/2 3/2 4/6 5/4 6/1 7/6 8/3 9/7 10/5 11/2 12/7 1/4/91

Investor's Business Daily

price in the handle (at Points C, D and E). While we call this a new high, it is actually a new high breaking out of the handle trading range, which is usually a little below the actual old high price at Point A. This gives you a slight jump or edge on the stock.

Why don't you just buy at the bottom of the cup?

People feel uncomfortable waiting for a specific buy point, especially because most of the time it is at a higher price than other prices in the basing area. They ask: "Why not buy earlier at a cheaper price in order to get a better deal? Why wait until it is up a few points higher before I buy?" The objective is not to buy at the cheapest price when the probability of the stock having a huge move may be only so-so. The objective is to buy at exactly the right time—the time when the chances are greatest that the stock will succeed and move up significantly. I found through our detailed historical studies that a stock purchased at this correct "pivot point," if all the other fundamental and technical factors of stock selection are in place, will simply not go down 8% (your protective sell rule), and has the greatest chance of moving substantially higher. So ironically, if done correctly, this is your point of least risk.

On the day the stock breaks out, its trading volume should increase at least 50% above its average daily trading volume. It is important to have big professional demand for your stock at this key buy point. Only *Investor's Business Daily*'s unique stock tables show you each stock's volume percent change daily.

On our chart, the dashed line from Points X to A is called the prior uptrend. Strong, healthy stocks show at least 30% price increases in their prior uptrend. A proper "cup with handle" must take at least seven or eight weeks to form (from Point A to Point E). Otherwise, it may be unsound and fail after its breakout. Some bases may actually be three, six or as many as fifteen months in duration. Most decline 20% to 30% from their absolute peak, to the low of the cup (from A to B). Handles can be a short (one or two weeks), or a number of weeks long, and need to drift downward along their price lows or have a shakeout (break below a prior week's price low in the handle). This serves the purpose of getting a needed pullback, or price correction, out of the way.

Proper handles rarely pull back in price more than 10% or 15%. They will usually show either a marked dry-up in volume near their lows, which means there is no more selling coming into the stock, or they will have several tight areas where the price varies only a tiny amount, and for several weeks may close virtually unchanged in price. This is a constructive signal.

Seems clear in theory, but do actual stocks really form such patterns?

Here's a classic example of a "cup with handle" pattern: Microsoft in January 1991, one week before it broke to new price highs and went on to more than double in price (see chart on page 46). Its EPS Rating was 99 and its Relative Price Strength Rating was 96 at the time. Microsoft formed a 25-week base. It declined six weeks on the downside from Point A, moved back and forth along the low of the cup at Point B, rallied up in November (Point C) and then formed a very tight handle (Points D, E) in the last five or six weeks. Note that the handle is in the upper half of the overall pattern (Points C, D, E).

I've placed arrows on six different weeks along the low and on the uptrend in the base where volume (shown on the bottom of the chart) increases from the week before with the price increasing. The two largest volume weeks were on big up weeks in price with the price closing at the peak for the week. Note also the extreme volume dry-up in December to the lowest weekly volume level on the chart and the small tight price movement in late December and early January.

Your precise buy point is the peak in the handle area. Again, this is not the lowest price, but the price at which your probability of being right is highest. That's why you wait for the stock to hit this price before you buy (sometimes they never get to this point).

Until you get used to it, it will seem scary, strange and hard to believe that the correct way to buy is when a stock is near the highest point it has ever been. In fact, 98% of individual investors never buy this way, and that's why few will ever own, or fully capitalize on, the really big new winners that occur year after year in the U.S. stock market. Just remember buying at new highs is buying into emerging strength.

SUMMARY

- In studying the greatest stock market winners over the past 45 years, I found specific types of base patterns. These bases were formed just before the stocks broke out into new high ground in price and then went on to make their biggest gains.

- The most common pattern is a "cup with handle" named so because it resembles a coffee cup when viewed from the side.

- The optimal buy point of any stock is its "pivot point," the point at the end of a basing area when the stock price is breaking out into new high ground.

- On the day a stock breaks out, volume should increase 50% above its average.

- Remember, you want to buy a stock when it is breaking into new high ground. 98% of individual investors never buy this way, and that's why few will ever own the big stock winners.

- Increased volume from the prior day/week with the price moving up is generally a positive sign.

- Increased volume from the prior day/week with the price moving down is generally a negative sign.

- A decrease in price on decreased volume indicates no significant selling.

LESSON 10

How Chart Patterns Lead to Big Profits

There are several different patterns to look for when doing technical analysis. In this lesson, Bill O'Neil discusses a couple different patterns and also goes over some mistakes to avoid when chart reading.

When did you realize the importance of reading charts?

I first discovered how critical charts were in 1959, one year after I became a stockbroker. At that time, there was one mutual fund that happened to be materially outperforming all others. I got a weekly chart book and posted from prospectuses and quarterly reports the price at which the fund purchased every new stock during the prior two years. I discovered something very important.

What I learned was so startling, it simply changed my whole view about how to pick winning stocks. Every single one of the approximately 100 new stocks the fund purchased was bought only after it bolted into new high ground in price! For example, if a stock had fluctuated back and forth between $40 and $50 for three to six months, this #1 fund only bought when the stock made a new high at $51.

Let's stop and think about this concept for a moment. The idea of buying a stock at the highest price it has ever sold for just as it is coming out of a correct basing area seems ludicrous. After all, most of us were raised with the idea of getting a deal, a bargain. I'm here to shatter a common and comfortable misconception.

What applies to buying merchandise on sale at a department store works in the completely opposite way when dealing with stocks. Do you want stocks that have the greatest potential for moving even higher? Then, you've got to ignore the erroneous old saying, "buy low and sell high," and replace it with "buy high and sell a lot higher."

It's all a matter of perspective and experience. Look back at a huge winner like Cisco Systems. From its original new high "pivot point" of $30 in October 1990 through October 1998, it has increased an incredible 15,650%. The original new high "pivot point" was actually low. It seemed high only because its price history was all that was known at that time. The incredible gains to come were not yet visible, so high is rarely high when you're looking for really great companies.

What are some other price patterns that emerge before stocks take off?

In addition to the common "cup with handle" pattern, see the graph on the next page for an example of a "double bottom" chart pattern.

Spotting The Double-Bottom

Here's how American Power Conversion set up before making an 800% gain in the following 22 months

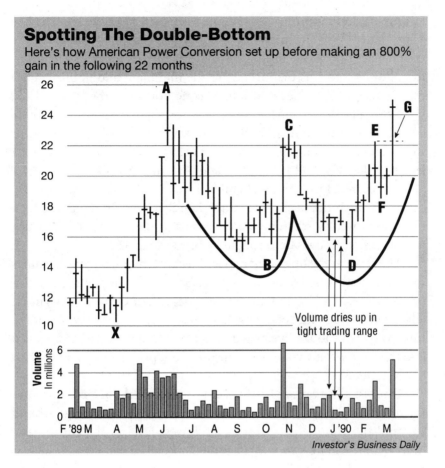

Volume dries up in tight trading range

Investor's Business Daily

American Power Conversion's 39-week pattern in 1990 looked like a large letter "W." The midpoint of the "W" at Point C should be below the high at Point A, the beginning of the pattern. A to B is the first bottom, Points B to C is the increase to the midpoint, and Points C to D represents the second leg down, the second bottom in the "W."

Normally, the second leg down will drop slightly below the absolute low of the first bottom at Point B. This serves as a shakeout and helps wear out, or scare out, the last few weak shareholders. D to E is the last leg up in the "W," and Points E, F, and G form a short handle.

The correct buy point is slightly above $22 at Point G, as the stock breaks through the peak price of the handle (Point E). Note the high increase in weekly trading volume shown at the bottom of the chart when the stock moves up through the breakout at $22.

The stock at the buy point had an *Investor's Business Daily* Earnings Per Share Rating of 99, a Relative Price Strength Rating of 95, a return on equity of 53.8% and a 25% annual pre-tax profit margin. It advanced 800% in the following 22 months from Point G, which at the time must have looked very high and scary to most investors. Notice also the huge weekly volume on the one week price run up from $18 to $22 at Point C.

One last observation: During the last three weeks of December and the first week in January, the stock closed in a very tight range around $17 and the volume dried up to the lowest level in the entire base. Most people will never spot this, but it is usually a constructive sign as the volume dry-up indicates there is no more selling coming into the market.

Any other price patterns to look for?

Another somewhat common pattern is the "flat base." It can occur after a stock has formed a "cup with handle" and has then continued to move up. Simply, the price pattern moves straight sideways and holds tight for at least five weeks, normally only correcting 8% to 12%. At the end of this type of pattern, a new "pivot point" is established, giving you a new chance to buy or add to your possible earlier "cup with handle" buy.

You want to buy a stock exactly at its "pivot point" as it breaks out of a sound pattern. Don't chase it up more than 5% past its pivot. If you do, you will be buying more extended in price. (It always pays to start exactly right and not be late.) Your risk of being shaken out on a normal price correction will substantially increase.

What are some mistakes you can make in reading charts, and is there such a thing as faulty base patterns?

1. Short bases of one to four weeks in duration are very risky and usually fail. Avoid them.

2. Patterns that are abnormally wide or loose in overall appearance are more risky. It's safer to buy tighter, better contained patterns with less wild price fluctuations.

3. Stocks that shoot up straight from the bottom of a pattern into new highs without any pullbacks or handles are risky and frequently have sharp sell-offs.

4. A base breakout with no real increase in volume should be avoided.

5. Laggard bases. The last stock in a group to break out to a new high is weak and a laggard. It should be passed up.

6. Handle areas that are too wide and loose (down 20% to 30%) or handles that wedge up along their lows rather than drift down along the lows are faulty and frequently fail.

7. After a stock has had a long advance, the fourth time the stock forms a base ("fourth stage" base) is usually too obvious to everyone and will probably fail (more on this in Lesson 11).

Once you learn to read charts and correctly recognize stocks with sound base patterns that are under accumulation and possess all of the fundamental earnings criteria we mentioned earlier in this book, your performance should improve significantly.

SUMMARY

- Some of the price patterns to look for when choosing stocks are the "cup with handle," "double bottom," and "flat base."
- There are faulty base patterns, so watch out for the following:

  1) abnormally wide or loose handles

  2) upward wedging handles

  3) wide or loose overall base patterns

  4) laggard stocks that are the last to form bases among stocks in their industry groups

  5) no increased volume during breakouts

  6) "fourth stage" bases

  7) short bases

- Replace the old adage, "buy low and sell high" with "buy high and sell a lot higher."
- You want to buy a stock at its exact "pivot point." Don't chase it up more than 5% past the pivot.

How to Read Stock Charts Like a Pro

Chart reading is one of the more difficult skills to master. In this lesson, Bill O'Neil gives specific examples and discusses the finer points of chart reading as well as exceptions to a few of the rules he has covered.

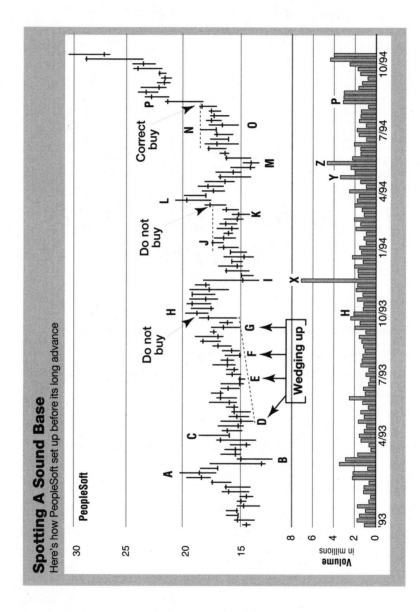

Spotting A Sound Base

Here's how PeopleSoft set up before its long advance

Some charts look good at the moment, but not all stocks go on to make big gains. How do you tell the difference between a sound base and a faulty one?

The real value of charts is in evaluating a stock's activity in relation to its recent past—its environment or setting. With all the factors that can affect the market, from the Fed and interest rates to international markets and politics, a stock chart, with its relatively simple price and volume lines—represents actual performance of a stock in the marketplace.

The PeopleSoft chart on the opposite page is a good example of how little details can make the difference between faulty bases, prone to failure, and sound bases that may be extremely profitable.

Points A, B, and C in 1993 appear to be the cup portion of a "cup with handle." However, the handle area from Points C to H is wedging upward along the low points at D, E, F and G. Each point inches up a little higher along the low points. Most bases that do this will fail after they break out, which this one did at Point H. Also note the weekly volume at the bottom of the chart was lower on the breakout week (Point H) than the prior week. This is another bad signal. The volume should increase on the breakout week when compared to the week before.

PeopleSoft built a second base from Points H to L. This time the handle area drifted down from Points J to K, which is better because it shakes out weak holders by undercutting the closing low prices of the prior few weeks. Handles, however, should not form in the lower half of the overall base, which this one did.

How do you measure to see if the handle is at the mid to upper part of the base vs. the lower part?

Take the pattern's absolute high price $19 7/8 (Point H) and the absolute low in the base of $13 (Point I), which is an overall decline of $6 7/8 points. Now take the peak in the handle of $17 (Point J) and the low of the handle, $14 (Point K). The midpoint in the handle is $15 1/2. Now, is $15 1/2 closer to the $19 7/8 high (Point H) or is it closer to the $13 low (Point I)? It's only 2 1/2 points off the low and is 4 3/8 points from the high.

The midpoint of the handle is closer to the lower half, a weak sign indicating a faulty base that you would not want to buy when it tries to break out (Point L). Note also the enormous volume selling week at Point X, when PeopleSoft broke below its support price of $15 established two months earlier.

It takes time to learn these intricacies. Even experienced chartists can get suckered into buying at Points H and L.

Where does PeopleSoft set up properly?

The stock finally forms a third, more proper "cup with handle," from Points L to P. The handle from Points N to O is a lot closer to the midpoint of the base. This base is much tighter and better contained than the first one. Four weeks down from Point L, the stock breaks below its $16 support of two weeks earlier, but on rather small volume. This is better than the enormous volume spike on the downside in base #2 at Week X.

Note also the big volume/price runup in Week Y, as well as the huge volume at Week Z. At first glance you might misread volume at Week Z as a negative sign. It's actually a sign of major support buying.

Here's how to interpret this action. For the two prior weeks, the stock closed down in price 1 1/4 to 1 1/2 points each week. The weekly volume then surges, but the stock only closes down 1/8. I call this "heavy volume without further price progress on the downside." It's big volume institutional buying support that stops the stock from continuing its decline and causes it to close virtually unchanged in price for the week. Now you have two of the prior four weeks showing big volume support along the lows of the pattern.

The correct buy point in this base is $18 1/2. Observe the extreme volume dry-up the week before the breakout (no one is watching the dull activity—it's not so obvious). Then, the breakout week brings a large volume increase at Point P.

This is the precise week where our institutional research firm, William O'Neil + Co., recommended PeopleSoft to its institutional clients as a buy in August 1994. The Earnings Per Share Rating then was 99 and the Relative Price Strength Rating was 87. PeopleSoft's pre-tax profit margins were 23.5% and its prior five-year earnings growth rate was 163%. Additionally, management owned 50% of the stock, the P/E ratio was 45 times earnings (it later sold at over 100 times earnings), and the average daily volume was 142,000 shares.

What other tips can help you find sound bases?

Most successful stocks, as they make their way up in price, build a number of bases, each one a different "stage" base. The first time a correct base is formed ("first stage"), few people recognize it. Generally, it's a stock most investors are unaware of, so few buy it. Some people see the second base, but by the time the third and especially the fourth bases are formed on a stock's long way up, it's so obvious, everybody sees it. The market moves to disappoint the masses and because most stocks that are obvious usually don't work, if you buy "fourth-stage" bases, you will be wrong 80% of the time. When a "fourth stage" base fails, it will undercut the prior low in the base. Frequently, fourth stage base failures coincide with important turndowns in the general market. If the stock later rebounds and begins making new bases, the bases "re-set" and you begin counting bases all over again.

Chart price and volume action can frequently help you recognize when a stock has reached its top and should be sold—much sooner than negative changes in earnings signal a problem. For example, when the oil service stocks topped in October 1980, most of them showed earnings up 100% or more and analyst estimates were terrific for the next several quarters. But the price and volume action showed heavy distribution (professional selling). This indicates the time to sell, no matter what the fundamentalists are saying.

I scan a chart book looking for sound patterns and stocks that fit the CAN SLIM formula discussed in my book, *How to Make Money in Stocks*. A sound base should usually have more weeks in which the price is up on greater-than-average volume than weeks down on greater-than-average volume. There also should be some tight weeks that show little price change. I like to see a huge weekly volume spike on weeks of price increase once or twice in the past twelve months of price and volume action.

Most big stock leaders, after they initially break out of a sound base, will go up 20% in eight weeks or less. Therefore, I would never want to sell a potential big leader that races up 20% in only one to four weeks.

Sixty percent of the time, leaders will not pull back to the point of their pivot (or buy) price. However, sometimes you can make an additional buy the first time a stock pulls back in price to its fifty-day moving average line.

I recommend you study charts and you'll start to recognize patterns. You'll discover things you never knew before about stocks and how they behave. Cut out and save patterns of really great performing stocks so you'll learn what to look for next time. History always repeats itself. Patterns that worked five, ten and fifteen years ago work just as well today because human nature and investor psychology never really change. One place to start reviewing charts is with Daily Graphs Online, found at www.dailygraphs.com.

Keep in mind that general market corrections are natural and normal adjustments, not something to panic or lose your confidence over; they help build another round of bases. Without corrections in the market, there would be a lot fewer correct "cup with handle" formations. It's the downturns that help create the left-hand side of the cup. It's really a matter of perspective. With strict selling rules in place and a solid way to interpret what the general market indices are doing, you can afford to sell some stock around a top and wait for a whole new round of future PeopleSoft patterns to form. In time they always do. These new patterns are something you can't afford to miss, so never let yourself get discouraged and give up during market corrections.

Summary

- Most successful stocks, as they make their way up in price, build a number of bases, each one a different "stage" base. Third and especially "fourth-stage" bases are prone to failure.

- Chart price and volume action frequently can help you recognize when a stock has reached its top and should be sold.

- Study chart patterns of past winning stocks. You'll be able to learn what to look for in the future. History always repeats itself in the market.

- Look for handles that form in the upper half of the base.

- A sound base should usually have more weeks where the price is up on greater-than-average volume than weeks down on greater-than-average volume.
- Most big stock market leaders breaking out of a sound base will go up 20% in eight weeks or less from the "pivot point." I never sell a stock that does this in four weeks or less.

How to Gauge the Stock Market's Health

To be a successful investor, understanding the market's direction is critical. In this lesson, Bill O'Neil will show you how to interpret the market's behavior.

From your experience, what would you say are the essential steps to successful investing?

If you are an individual investor, whether new or experienced, and you want to make money and perform well investing in common stocks, there are just three key steps you must learn and follow.

- First, you have to develop buying selection rules that let you pick the best stocks, and use charts to determine the right time to buy.

- Second, you must have a set of selling rules that tell you when to sell and nail down a profit, or cut short a loss to avoid a possible larger loss.

- And third, you need a specific method to tell you when the general market averages are topping and headed down, and when they've finally hit bottom and turned into a new uptrend. That's all you need.

What is the general market, and why is it important for you to understand it? Why can't you just buy a good stock and forget about it?

The general market is represented by leading market indices like the S&P 500, Dow Jones Industrials and the Nasdaq Composite. The reason you need to carefully evaluate these indices is that when they top, then turn down and go into a significant decline, three out of four stocks (whether you think they're good or bad) will follow the market's trend and also decline in price.

Many growth stocks, secondary, lower-quality companies in an industry, and even certain high-tech stocks can drop two to three times as much as the market averages. And worse still, some of them might not come back up or could take years to do so. So if a bear market declines 20% to 25% (a somewhat normal bear market correction from its absolute top), some of your stocks could drop 40% to 75% from their peak price.

It's of no value to make a worthwhile gain during several years of a bull (up) cycle and then give it all back during the following bear (down) cycle. It's better to get out of the elevator on one of the floors on the way up than to ride it all the way back down. It usually takes investors at least three or four years to learn this lesson the hard way. So you have to learn to both buy stocks at the right time *and* to sell them at the right time.

Why do some bear markets last only a few months while others drag on for years?

Since I've been investing, I've lived through twelve bear markets and have carefully analyzed eighteen of them going back to the turn of the century. Basic conditions in the U.S. and the world usually determine the length and depth of a bear market.

When the U.S. is in real trouble, you tend to get corrections of 30% to 50% in the Dow Industrials. That happened in 1937 (a Depression year), 1940–1942 (start of World War II), 1966, 1969–1970, 1973–1974 and 1977 (years of Vietnam, gold flowing out of the country, OPEC oil price increases, Soviet Union expansionism, rampant inflation and 20% interest rates during the Carter era).

When basic conditions in America are not as bad, like in 1948–1949, 1953, 1957, 1960, 1980, 1982, 1990 and 1998, you get smaller market declines of around 17% to 27% off the peak.

Strangely, many of these declines end in the fourth quarter of the year. Bear markets are normal and necessary and serve to clean up prior excesses. They also allow the market to create a whole new set of chart bases and leaders for the bull market that, in time, always follows. So, never let yourself get discouraged or lose your confidence; otherwise, you'll miss the next bull market.

The experts never seem to agree about the market. How do you tell who's right?

I don't listen to any personal opinions about the market but instead study the day-to-day price and volume changes in the leading indices. I'm not trying to predict the market into the distant future but merely to understand its exact condition at the time—day by day. Is it in a confirmed up or downtrend, and is it acting in a normal or abnormal manner? We put all the important market indices on one convenient page in

Investor's Business Daily, the "General Market & Sectors" page, which I check every single day.

The three key indices are stacked, one on top of the other, to help you spot divergences in action at key turning points. For example, one index may drop to new lows while another, broader index (such as Nasdaq), may diverge and hold above its prior low, indicating strength in a wider part of the market and weakness in another. *Investor's Business Daily* has also placed its mutual fund index on this page because it has, at times, been an excellent general market indicator. *Investor's Business Daily* also has a one-of-a-kind column called "The Big Picture." It will help you learn how to decipher the many changes that happen in the various indicators on the "General Market & Sectors" page.

I have personally found the dozens of other technical market tools (followed by most technicians) to be far less reliable than just watching the behavior of the key market averages daily and the action of individual stock leaders.

SUMMARY

- The general market is represented by leading market indices like the S&P 500, Dow Jones Industrials, and the Nasdaq Composite. Tracking the general market is key because most stocks follow the trend of the general market.

- Ignore personal opinions about the market. Instead, study the day-to-day price and volume changes in the leading indices.

- *Investor's Business Daily*'s "General Market & Sectors" page will help you understand what is going on now in the general market. "The Big Picture" column will help unravel its complexity.

- A typical bear market will decline 20% to 25% from its peak price. A negative political or economic environment could cause a more severe decline.

How to Spot When the Market Hits a Top

The market is perhaps the most important, but least understood, element in investing. In this lesson, Bill O'Neil explains the details of a market index and what signs to look for when the market is hitting a top.

Knowing *when* to buy or sell a stock is key. Lesson 1 of this book is dedicated to why individual stock investors should always, without exception, cut every loss when down 8% below the price paid for a stock.

A man wrote to us and said he'd read my book, *How to Make Money in Stocks*, and agreed with the methods discussed, but didn't agree with the loss-cutting rule. To make any method work, you have to develop the strict discipline to follow all of the rules, not just the ones you find agreeable. Most investors have trouble believing all of the principles of sound investing. It takes losing hard-earned cash before they start to understand that stocks are highly speculative and can easily decline a lot more than 8%. Bernard Baruch, a well-known financier, said, "You don't have to be right all the time in the market; in fact you could make a fortune only being right 50% of the time as long as you have the sense to always cut short your losses."

Because three out of four stocks, regardless of how "good" they are, will eventually follow the trend of the general market, it is important to learn how to spot when the market is hitting a top.

After four or five days of distribution (selling), the general market will normally turn down. Using this approach, it was fairly easy to spot the top in the 1998 bull market. (See the top chart on page 71.)

In general, distribution is indicated by the index closing down on increased volume or a day's attempted advance stalling (very little change in price) on greater volume than the day before. On April 22, (the top chart on page 71) the Dow closed down slightly from the prior day's close. (The daily close is indicated by the short horizontal slash mark in the vertical daily line.) The NYSE volume at the bottom of the chart increased from the day before. That's day one of distribution. Three days later at Point 2, the Dow declined badly and the volume again increased from the day before. That's day two of distribution. Six days later, at Point 3, the Dow closed down with that day's volume up. The very next day, Point 4, the sell-off accelerated on increased volume, and you had the fourth day of distribution.

Four days of distribution, if correctly spotted over a two- or three-week period, are often enough to turn a previously advancing market into a decline. Sometimes distribution could be spread over six or seven weeks if the market attempts to rally back to new highs. When I see four clear distribution days, I will start looking for stocks that are giving indi-

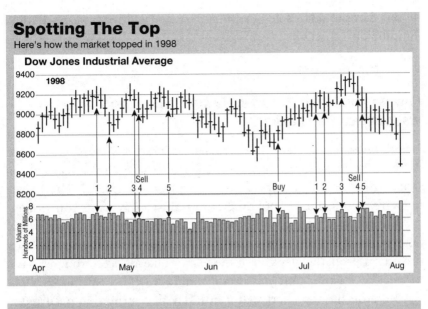

Spotting The Top

Here's how the market topped in 1998

Dow Jones Industrial Average

1998

Sell

Buy

Sell

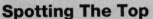

Volume Hundreds of Millions

Apr   May   Jun   Jul   Aug

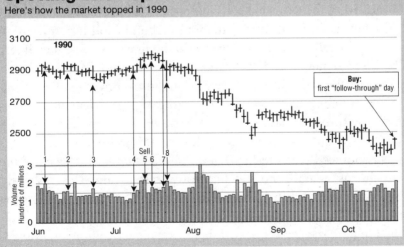

Spotting The Top

Here's how the market topped in 1990

1990

Buy:
first "follow-through" day

Sell

Volume Hundreds of millions

Jun   Jul   Aug   Sep   Oct

cations they should be sold or trimmed back. (I will go through sell rules for individual stocks in Lessons 20 and 21.)

How do you learn to correctly spot these days of distribution on the Dow?

I check *Investor's Business Daily*'s "General Market & Sectors" page every day because I don't want to miss the few days when these distribution signals may suddenly appear with no prior warning. To be naive, unaware, uninformed or not on the job almost always costs you money.

Anyone can learn how to spot distribution days. How long will it take you to do it well? Ask yourself: How long did it take to learn how to drive a car properly, play golf or the piano? Like any skill, you just have to practice and over time you steadily improve.

Note on the top chart that a fifth day of distribution occurred a week later (Point 5) on May 15. Once you see these signs, you should stop all buying and even cut back your positions. From some later point, the market average will always attempt to rebound and turn upward— this we call a rally. Don't get drawn into the first or second day of any rally, after you have seen four or five definite distribution days. It could be a false rally. The market is now turning into a downtrend, and you don't want to buy anything until the market signals a clear and powerful "follow-through" day, which usually occurs between the fourth and seventh day of an attempted rally. (More on this in Lesson 14.)

Now notice Point 1 in July 1998. Volume is up for the day, but the Dow churns, making no net headway. It stalls and closes slightly down—day one of distribution. Two days later at Point 2 it does the same thing. The market average breaks down with volume up. Four days later (Point 3), the Dow closes off slightly on higher volume. At Point 4, the Dow closes badly on increased volume.

Again you have the fourth day of distribution, and it's selling time. If you're invested on margin (using borrowed money), your risk can be twice as great—so sell and get off margin, otherwise you can get seriously hurt. The market is telling you this is when you should be fearing, not hoping. The next day (Point 5) volume escalates further and you're into a headlong decline.

There is no reason for individual investors to be fully invested in stocks from that top to the ultimate market bottom if they had studied and used this method. Markets never go down by accident. The information and signals are always there. Sadly, ignorance, ego, pride, wishful thinking, vacillation and unrealistic hoping usually prevent people from objectively analyzing the market averages and making sell decisions correctly.

These topping patterns seem to show up again and again.

That's correct. Here's one last example (the bottom chart on page 71) that should further clarify how you properly evaluate the market's direction. This, along with your *Investor's Business Daily*, should be worth a lot of dollars to you if you'll buckle down, study and learn how to take advantage of these clear-cut signals.

Point 1 in June 1990 was the first day of distribution during the uptrend of the previous month. Point 2 shows the Dow stalling and barely closing down with just a slight increase in volume. But it still indicates a second day of distribution. At Point 3, the Dow closes down sharply on a big jump in volume. Eleven days later at Point 4, the Dow is down on more volume.

At Point 5, the Dow actually stalls and closes up slightly for the day, but the net gain is significantly less than the net gain on the prior two days of big increases in the Dow. Also, it closes in the lower part of that day's spread (from high to low) on enormous volume. (The key here is the Dow index moves up much less than the day before while increased large volume occurs.)

This is how you analyze the law of supply and demand at work each day in this market index. It's detailed. It's important. And, it's also something few people understand or take the time to learn.

Why is it important? Simple. If you don't understand how to interpret this market action, you'll just lose a lot more money because you've missed a clear selling opportunity. Points 6, 7 and 8 are the remaining days of distribution across the 1990 market top. The Dow then turned down into a bear market decline of 22%. Anyone observing these eight days would have sold some stock. When the next attempted rally or two failed, they would have sold some more. I was completely out of this market by August 1, 1990 and avoided serious losses.

Every rally attempt failed until the first valid "follow-through" day occurred on the fifth day of the attempted rally in October. At that time, it was once again safe to re-enter the market and begin to buy.

SUMMARY

- Knowing when to both buy and sell a stock is key.

- Because three out of four stocks, regardless of how "good" they are, will eventually follow the trend of the general market, it is important to learn how to spot when the market is hitting a top.

- After four or five days of distribution within a two- to three-week period, the general market will normally turn down.

- Distribution is indicated by the index closing down on increased volume or a day's attempted advance stalling on greater volume than the day before. At this time, review the stocks in your portfolio and look for individual selling signs that indicate you should cut back or sell them.

LESSON 14

How to Spot When the Market Bottoms

Bill O'Neil constantly emphasizes that the best time to get back into the market is after a correction or bear cycle at the moment the market starts uptrending again. In order to do this, it is essential to be able to spot a market bottom. In this lesson, Bill O' Neil discusses the signs to look for to detect a market bottom.

Is it really important to know exactly when the market is turning up?

Bear markets create fear, uncertainty and a loss of confidence. When stocks hit bottom and turn up to begin the next bull market—loaded with opportunities—most people simply don't believe it. They're hesitant and afraid. Why? Most new investors, even professionals, are still licking their wounds. Without a system of cutting losses, or a way to interpret general market action, most people lose money and get hurt during market corrections.

Right when the next market cycle's big new winners are marching up to the starting gate, getting ready to run the race of their lives, investors freeze up because they're scared and because they don't follow a system or a set of sound rules. So they rely on their emotions and personal opinions, which are totally worthless at critical turning points like a major market bottom. The market's opinion is the only one ever worth following at this crucial time.

So how do you recognize when the market has bottomed and is ready to begin an exciting new bull cycle? On pages 77 and 78, I walk you through how the Dow bottomed in 1998. I also have included on pages 79 and 80 examples of major market bottoms during the past twenty years. Study them carefully. With knowledge and understanding, you'll gain confidence and get better results.

How do you tell when the market is definitely turning up for real?

At some point on the way down, the indices will attempt to rebound or rally. Bear markets normally come in two or three waves, interrupted by several attempted false rallies that usually fizzle out after one, two or three weeks and occasionally five to six weeks or more.

Eventually, after almost every stock has broken down and sold off in price and enough bad news and time has passed, the market finds real support. One of these attempted rallies will finally "follow-through," showing real power, indicated by one of the indices (Dow, S&P 500 or Nasdaq Composite) closing up 1% or more for the day, with a jump in volume from the day before.

You can't tell much on the first or second day of a rally, with all its

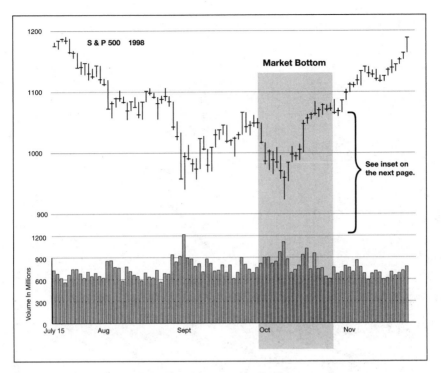

The 1998 Market Bottom

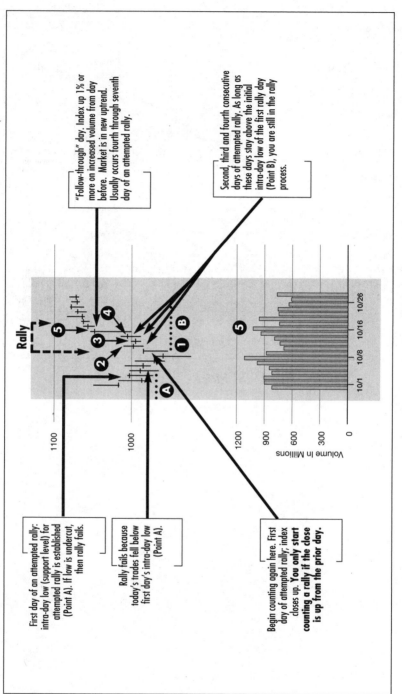

"Follow-through" day. Index up 1% or more on increased volume from day before. Market is in new uptrend. Usually occurs fourth through seventh day of an attempted rally.

Second, third and fourth consecutive days of attempted rally. As long as these days stay above the initial intra-day low of the first rally day (Point B), you are still in the rally process.

First day of an attempted rally: intra-day low (support level) for attempted rally is established (Point A). If low is undercut, then rally fails.

Rally fails because today's trades fell below first day's intra-day low (Point A).

Begin counting again here. First day of attempted rally; index closes up. **You only start counting a rally if the close is up from the prior day.**

The 1998 Market Bottom

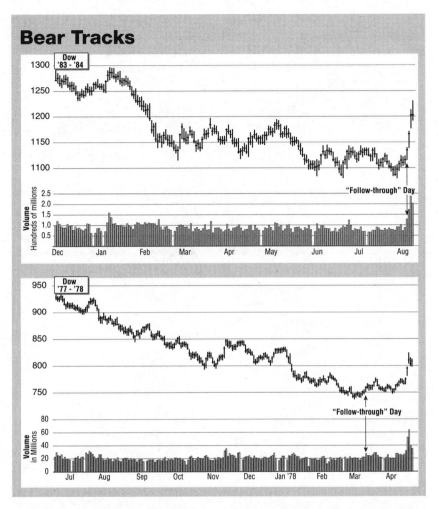

Bear Tracks

Dow '83 - '84

A 1% rise in a major index on higher volume than the prior day–also called a "follow-through" day–always confirms the bottom turn-around of a bear market.

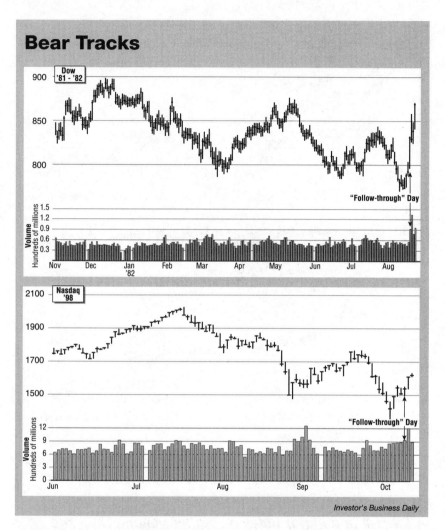

Bear Tracks

Investor's Business Daily

A 1% rise in a major index on higher volume than the prior day—also called a "follow-through" day—always confirms the bottom turn-around of a bear market.

exuberance, so it's best not to act upon them. The rally has yet to prove itself and still may be false. The market often settles back for a day or two but holds above its low or support level. The rally's support level is the lowest trading price of the first day of the rally. If it comes on again with clearly overwhelming power, you have a valid "follow-through" day, otherwise known as a confirmation of the turn. It usually occurs on the fourth through the seventh day of the attempted rally. "Follow-throughs" after the tenth day indicate the turn may be acceptable, but somewhat weaker.

I check the Dow Jones Industrials, the S&P 500 and the Nasdaq Composite indices on *Investor's Business Daily*'s "General Market & Sectors," page every day. An initial "follow-through" can occur on any one of the indices and is usually followed a few days later on another index. I have never missed the very beginning of a new bull market with this method of tracking the general market indices carefully.

About 20% of the time they can give a false buy signal, which is fairly easy to recognize after a few days, because the market will usually promptly and noticeably fail on large volume.

The reason for false signals? A huge institutional investor knowing this method can run up a few of the Dow stocks, or a few big high-tech leaders in the Nasdaq, and create a false impression of a valid "follow-through" day, especially if the market moves up on some seemingly good news that day. However, most true "follow-throughs" will usually show strong positive action on good volume either the day after the "follow-through" or several days later. At any rate, convincing power and strength is what you want to observe.

Markets usually discount news items and look ahead of the economy—up to six months in advance. Don't make your decisions based on your opinion of the news. Make it on the objective observation of when and how the general market indices finally change direction from their downward trend. Markets are rarely wrong; people's opinions and fears are frequently wrong.

What should investors look at first on the "General Market & Sectors" page?

I would rank day-to-day evaluation of the three key indices, plus *Investor's Business Daily*'s Mutual Fund Index, as the first to consider.

This is important because the Mutual Fund Index tracks the performance of some of the best money managers in the market. It shows how leading funds are faring and can give clues to the general market's health.

After these four indices (the Dow, S&P 500, Nasdaq and Mutual Fund Indices), next in importance would be observing the behavior and action of the leading stocks in the market. Are they acting normally or abnormally? Have the majority of them topped? This is really all you need, but it takes some study and experience to get it down accurately.

Of the remaining market variables, I would list changes in the Federal Reserve Board's discount rate (or Fed Funds Rate) next in importance. The discount rate is what it costs member banks to borrow money from the Fed. Logically, a cut in the rate encourages borrowing and increases money supply, whereas a hike in the rate does the opposite.

A lowering in the rate can generally signal a new bull market. But this indicator is not as reliable as really knowing how to interpret the market index changes. For example, two bull markets developed with no Fed rate cuts, and three times (in 1957, 1960 and 1981) the Fed lowered rates and the market continued to go down.

What about the psychological indicators? Are any of these useful?

There are a couple of psychological indicators that gauge mass opinion about the market. These are next in importance. They are the percentage of investment advisers who are bullish or bearish and the ratio of put volume to call volume, both found on the "General Market & Sectors" page. These indicators are generally contrarian.

Take the Put-Call Ratio. Stock option players buy calls in hopes that a stock will go up in price and puts if they think prices will fall. But option investors are historically wrong at key turning points about the market's direction. When they're extremely bearish, the Put-Call Ratio shoots up. That's when their excessive negativity signals a market upturn.

What are some other ways to use the "General Market & Sectors" page?

During attempted rallies in a bear market, the Advance/Decline Line (produced by taking all NYSE stocks that rise in price for the day and subtracting those that fall) can sometimes be of value, when it shows no ability to rebound when the indices try to rally.

However, *Investor's Business Daily*'s Mutual Fund Index can be used in the same way. For example, in August 1998, it hovered near its closing lows for three days while, at the same time, the Dow Jones Industrial Average attempted to rally near its upper range, but later promptly dropped rapidly.

I do not use the Advance/Decline Line at other times because it has frequently been known to give premature signals, way before a market's eventual top. It also can show false weakness at some bottoms when the market is actually turning up.

There are dozens of other popular general market technical indicators that are of limited use. I've found them to be subject to frequent misinterpretation, faulty or just plain confusing. And the last thing you ever want to do in the market is get confused.

I stick to the few key ones mentioned above. Overbought/Oversold Indicators, the total number of new high prices vs. new low prices, up-down volume or on-balance volume, buying power vs. selling pressure, moving averages and trend lines are mainly a waste of time and an unnecessary distraction, based on my research and experience over the years. They could mislead you and cost you a lot of money.

Need additional motivation to learn how to correctly spot market bottoms and the next new bull market? New big winners emerge during the first ten to fifteen weeks of a new bull market. Cisco Systems emerged from a new base off the bear market bottom in 1990 and zoomed 15,650%. Franklin Resources bolted forward off the 1984 bear market and raced ahead 14,900%. Home Depot, then also an unknown new name, broke out at $20 with a price-to-earnings ratio of 58 in September 1982 and proceeded to climb 37,900%.

Wal-Mart came out of the 1980 20% market sell-off and went on to soar over 13,300%. I began buying Pic'n'Save in late 1976 and held it for 7 1/2 years and a twentyfold advance. It really got going coming off the bottom of the 1978 bear market. And another, Price Co., had a tenfold move in 3 1/2 years, right off the bottom of the 1982 bear market.

More recently, coming off the market bottom in October 1998, I bought AOL and Charles Schwab. AOL went up 456% from the "pivot" or buy point and Schwab went up 313%. You simply cannot afford to miss out on the tremendous new investment opportunities that occur when the market finally turns up and gives a valid buy signal.

The United States presents a never-ending cycle of entrepreneurial opportunities, so never let yourself get discouraged. If the market kicks you around and you suffer some reversals, that's good. Study what you did wrong, learn from it, write out a better set of buy and sell rules, and don't you ever miss the beginning of each new bull market. If you're prepared and still reading your *Investor's Business Daily*, the opportunities of a lifetime will be right in front of your eyes when each new market cycle begins.

SUMMARY

- Bear markets create fear and uncertainty. When stocks hit bottom and turn up to begin the next bull market loaded with opportunities, most people simply don't believe it.

- At some point on the way down, the indices will attempt to rebound or rally. A rally is an attempt by a stock or the general market to turn up and advance in price after a period of decline.

- Bear markets normally come in two or three waves, interrupted by several attempted "false" rallies that usually fizzle out after one to three weeks and occasionally five to six weeks or more.

- Eventually, one of the rallies will "follow-through." A "follow-through" occurs when one of the indices closes up 1% or more with a jump in volume from the day before. This confirmation will usually happen on the fourth to tenth day of the attempted rally.

- The Dow, S&P 500, and Nasdaq indices, along with the IBD Mutual Fund Index are your best sources for analyzing the market's condition and determining if a top or bottom has occurred. Also, observing how leading stocks are acting can be another indicator of a market top.

- Most technical market indicators are of little value. Psychological indicators like the Put-Call Ratio can help confirm changes in the market's direction.

LESSON 15

Putting the Stock-Picking Puzzle Together

In this lesson, Bill O'Neil discusses how to thoroughly evaluate a stock before making a purchase.

I have numerous rules for selecting stocks. These rules come solely from studying extensive models of all successful companies every year since 1953.

Sixty percent of my method is devoted to fundamental analysis because I want to buy only really great companies that have unique new products or superior services. I'm looking for the true market leaders, companies that are #1 in their particular fields, companies that are superior to their competition or have little true competition. Once you determine that you are operating in an uptrending general market, here are the factors you should consider:

1. Is the company's current quarterly earnings per share up at least 25%? Are the percentage increases in profits accelerating compared to recent quarters? Does it have six to twelve quarters of significant earnings increases up 50%, 100%, even 200% or more? Is the next quarter's consensus earnings estimate up a worthwhile amount? Have earnings in the past few quarters been higher than expected? If it's a growth stock, is each of the last three years of earnings up an average of 25% or more per year? Is the company's Earnings Per Share Rating 80 or higher?

2. If it's a turnaround stock, does it have two quarters of strong earnings increases or one quarter that is up so much that the twelve months earnings per share are back to their old peak? If two or more quarters have turned up, are the trailing twelve-month earnings near or above the peak of the prior couple of years? How much are the consensus earnings estimates up for the next two years?

3. Does the company have six to twelve quarters of strong sales growth? And has that growth rate accelerated in recent quarters?

4. Is the current quarter's after-tax profit margin at or close to its peak? Has there been a general trend of profit-margin improvement over many quarters? Are the company's margins among the best in its industry?

5. Is the annual pre-tax profit margin 18% or more? (It's O.K. if retailers have lower margins.)

6. Is the return on equity 20% to 50% or more and is its ROE among the very best in its industry?

7. Is its Sales + Profit Margins + ROE Rating an A or B? That would place it among the top 40% of all stocks in terms of sales growth, pre-tax and after-tax profit margins, and return on equity.

8. Does the company's management own the stock?

9. Is the stock in a quality price range? Quality comes at $16 to $150 for Nasdaq stocks and $20 and above for NYSE stocks. Remember, real leaders like Cisco Systems, Wal-Mart, Microsoft, PeopleSoft and Amgen broke out of their beginning chart bases several years ago between $30 and $50 per share—before they had giant price advances. Price is a basic reflection of quality. Quality doesn't come cheap.

10. Is the stock part of a historically winning industry group such as retail, computers and technology, drug and health care, or leisure and entertainment? Is it in one of the top five groups now? Check the "52-Week Highs & Lows" feature ("New Highs" list) on the "Industry Groups" page for the top five performing groups.

11. Do *Investor's Business Daily*'s small index charts on the "Industry Groups" page show that the current market favors big-cap or small-cap stocks? You want to go with the flow and not fight current market trends.

12. What broad economic sector is the market favoring? Consumer or high-tech? Growth or cyclical (stocks that move up and down with the business cycle), or defensive (food, utilities and other things everyone uses all the time)? Newer issues or older, more established companies?

13. Does the company's product save money, solve a problem or save time with new technology? Or is it a new drug or medical technique? Is it widely needed or liked? Is it a product that encourages repeat sales?

14. Is the company's backlog of unfilled orders expanding? At what percent of capacity is the company operating? What is the company's expected rate of future expansion?

15. Have one or two of the smarter, better-performing mutual funds bought the stock recently? This is an indirect, fundamen-

tal cross-check because the better institutions will have done extensive research before buying.

16. Do you really understand and believe in the company's business? Have you seen or used its product or service? The more you know about your company, the more conviction you'll have.

Now that you're dealing with a truly superior company, the remaining 40% is technical and timing analysis. You need *both*—not just one or the other. A big league pitcher needs more than a good fastball; he also needs a curve, a change-up and, most of all, great control and discipline. Successful investors need more than one tool as well.

1. Check a daily chart service, such as Daily Graphs or Daily Graphs Online, to spot which of your prospects are forming a sound pattern and are under accumulation (professional buying). They must also be near a proper buy point.

   Analyze the week-by-week price and volume action. Write down the price at which you will begin buying the stock. After your initial purchase, identify a price area at which you will add a small amount as a follow-up buy if it continues to perform well. I usually add more once a stock is up 2 1/2% to 3% from my first buy.

   If the stock drops 8% below your exact initial buy point, protect yourself against a possible larger loss by selling at the current market price. This loss-cutting discipline will, in the long run, keep you out of serious trouble.

2. You want an increase of 50% or more in trading volume on the day you begin buying with the stock breaking out of a sound base.

3. Is the chart pattern a "cup with handle," "double bottom" or "flat base"? If it's not any of these, it may be faulty and failure-prone.

4. Is its Relative Price Strength Rating 80 or more? And is the relative strength line on the chart in a definite uptrend?

5 Portfolio management: Keep and try to add to your best-performing stocks and reduce or sell your worst-acting ones.

And remember, stocks in sound base patterns and near new highs in price are better than stocks nearing or at new low prices.

6. Check a long-term monthly chart to see if the stock is also emerging out of a long-term base over a number of years.

SUMMARY

- Once you determine you are operating in an uptrending general market, you need to pick superior stocks.

- Potential winners will have strong earnings and sales growth, increasing profit margins and high return on equity (17% or more). They also should be in a leading industry group.

- *Investor's Business Daily*'s proprietary data and the IBD *SmartSelect*™ Corporate Ratings will help you pick winning stocks.

LESSON 16

How to Find New Investment Ideas in Investor's Business Daily

Investor's Business Daily *is much more than just a newspaper. It is a research tool. In the following discussion, Bill O'Neil shows you how he finds winning investment ideas in* Investor's Business Daily.

Where's a good place to start in Investor's Business Daily each day?

First you should scan the short summary, "The Markets," with the prior day's closing prices of the S&P 500 and the Dow Jones Industrials, as well as the Nasdaq and NYSE volume—all found on the front page each day. This will help you quickly gauge the movement of the general market. "IBD's Top 10" stories on the front page and "To the Point" found on Page A2 are designed to give the busy reader a quick, time-saving review of all the key business news of the day. It's worth checking, particularly if you don't have time to read the morning paper and are tired of the evening news.

Next, you may want to cut out and save "The New America" page. It has stories of exciting, newer entrepreneurial companies you may want to refer to in the future. This is where a number of major stock market winners originally were profiled. When the market is favoring the technology sector, *Investor's Business Daily*'s "Computers & Technology" page can help you keep up on the best companies in these industries.

Be absolutely certain you study the "How to Use IBD *SmartSelect*™ Corporate Ratings" box found at the beginning of the main NYSE and Nasdaq stock tables. This is a must read. It will help you better use and understand all of *Investor's Business Daily*'s proprietary measurements that screen out deficient stocks and identify the best market leaders.

The IBD *SmartSelect*™ Corporate Ratings consist of five proprietary ratings. The first is the Earnings Per Share (EPS) Rating. Second, is the Relative Price Strength (RS) Rating. These first two ratings are shown on a relative scale from 1 to 99, with 99 being the best. The EPS Rating and RS Rating should *both* normally be 80 or higher. You don't want one higher and one lower. This would indicate that a stock is at least in the top 20% of all stocks in terms of its vital earnings growth record and relative price action over the past year.

The third is the Industry Group Relative Strength Rating, which rates a stock's industry group price action over the past six months. You will have a better chance of succeeding if you stick to stock purchases among leading groups and sectors.

Fourth is the Sales + Profit Margins + ROE (SMR) Rating, which combines four fundamental measurements (sales growth, before- and after-tax profit margins, and return on equity) into one easy rating.

The fifth rating is the Accumulation/Distribution Rating, which identifies whether a stock is under professional buying or selling over the last 13 weeks.

The last three ratings are provided on an easy-to-use scale from A to E. For Industry Group Relative Strength Rating and the SMR Rating, an A would indicate the top 20% of the market in terms of these variables, B the top 40%, and so on. For the Accumulation/Distribution Rating, the scale has a slightly different meaning: An A or B indicates heavy or moderate professional buying, C indicates a neutral amount of buying and selling, and D or E indicates moderate or heavy selling.

How should an investor use Investor's Business Daily's ratings and stock tables?

You generally want to avoid companies where the EPS Rating and RS Rating are each less than 70. There are probably much better choices in stocks with higher ratings. Likewise, if a stock has a couple of Ds or Es, there are probably better choices available. The best companies should probably show at least a B on all three ratings.

I scan the main NYSE and Nasdaq tables every day, looking at all the boldfaced stocks (indicating stocks up $1 or more for the day or making a new price high), checking the company name, closing price, net change and volume percentage change. I circle any interesting names that I may want to research further. This daily scan keeps me aware and on top of all significant new stock movements.

You also want to check the "52-Week Highs & Lows" feature ("New Highs" list) every day on the "Industry Groups" page to identify the strongest stocks in the leading five industry groups in the market right now. Additionally, the "Best Ups" list in *Investor's Business Daily*'s earnings section is a good place to look for companies reporting large earnings increases.

Each day, you should study the "Where the Big Money's Flowing" list located at the beginning of the NYSE and Nasdaq stock tables. These are sophisticated screens that flag the better companies that are up or down for the day on a big jump in trading volume. Unusual trading volume signals the flow of big institutional money into or out of a stock. For further information on stocks that the leading mutual funds may have taken new positions in, I survey the bar charts on the "Mutual Funds" page in *Investor's Business Daily* every day.

What about the small stock charts found throughout the paper?

I scan *Investor's Business Daily*'s "Stocks in the News" mini-charts located in the main NYSE and Nasdaq sections. These are weekly price charts of stocks either making new highs in price, approaching new highs, or those with large increases in volume. I circle the ones with price patterns that look sound. (Refer back to Lessons 9, 10 and 11 for examples of sound chart patterns.)

I then do further research on some of these companies and also use a chart service to help me know if the timing is right to buy any of the prospects I discover in *Investor's Business Daily*. We have a comprehensive chart service, Daily Graphs®, which is available online at www.dailygraphs.com®.

In every Friday issue, you shouldn't miss "Your Weekend Review." This is a virtual laundry list of all stocks that have both an EPS Rating and Relative Price Strength Rating of 85 or higher (top 15% of stocks in the entire market). The list is presented in order of industry group performance. This list will help you quickly identify the best stocks in the top industry groups. You'll also find 28 of these companies charted every Friday as well.

SUMMARY

- You generally want to avoid companies where the EPS Rating and RS Rating are each less than 70. Likewise, if a stock has a couple of Ds or Es, there are probably better choices available. The best companies should probably show at least a B on all three ratings.

- Look for stocks in the stock tables with boldfaced type. This indicates that a stock is up $1 or more for the day or is making a new price high. This might be a good starting point for further research.
- Using a chart service can help you determine if the timing is right to buy any of the prospects found in *Investor's Business Daily*.

LESSON 17

Growth vs. Value Investing

Broadly speaking, there are two types of investors: growth stock investors and value investors. Often, these two are pitted against each other, with each represented as the best way to invest.

What is the difference between growth and value investing?

Growth stock investors seek companies that show consistent earnings and sales growth, usually 20% or more each year for the past three or five years. Companies such as Schering-Plough, Paychex, Cisco Systems and Microsoft would be considered growth stocks in the 1990s. The price-to-earnings ratios of growth stocks are generally higher than those of the average stock simply because they have a record of better-than-normal earnings growth.

Typically, growth stocks have a high-quality, repeat-type product or service that generates superior profit margins and a return on equity of at least 17% to 50%. In addition, consensus earnings estimates for these stocks for the following year or two are also up a significant amount.

Value investors, on the other hand, search for stocks they believe are undervalued. These investors evaluate a company's balance sheet and profit-and-loss statement, looking for signs of hidden value—such as an unusually large amount of cash in the company or property carried on the books at cost, which is below the current market value, etc.

They are looking for a bargain and like to buy stocks with a low P/E ratio or a low price-to-book value.

They look to buy a business franchise at a low price. Value investors have to wait for the market to hopefully recognize their stock's value for it to go up in price. This usually takes a longer amount of time, and sometimes it doesn't happen at all.

Buying stocks with low P/E ratios seems to be a common practice. Aren't bargains good?

In general, the stock market is a free auction marketplace where most stocks sell for around the price they're actually worth at the time. In other words, a stock with a P/E ratio of 10 is worth 10 times its earnings, and a stock with a P/E ratio of 35 is worth 35 times its earnings. If and when the price or P/E ratio moves up or down, it is caused by continued improvement or deterioration in earnings reports.

So it's really improper to say a stock is a bargain because its P/E is low, and conversely, it's improper to say a stock with a high P/E is overpriced. You can't buy a Mercedes for a Chevrolet's price, nor can you get Mark McGwire, baseball's home-run king, for the salary of a .200 hitter.

The moral: You get what you pay for. The best company in an industry almost always sells at a much higher P/E than the also-rans in the group.

We built models of all the outstanding stocks during the 1990s—stocks like Amgen, Cisco Systems, Microsoft, America Online, Ascend, EMC and PeopleSoft. At the very beginning of their 500% to 1,000% advances, their P/Es averaged 31 times earnings. And most of these leaders, on average, expanded their P/Es to the low 70s as they had their huge price increases.

A value investor would have missed every one of these absolutely outstanding companies during their period of greatest performance. P/Es in my view are misused, misunderstood and overstated as a stock selection tool. Growth in earnings and sales is the fundamental cause behind almost all price advances.

If you choose to invest in individual stocks and you're not a professional investor, I firmly believe it is better for you to avoid the value approach and learn to invest in the very best growth companies. Buy corporations that *lead* their particular industries in sales, earnings, profit margins, and return on equity. Buy companies that are gaining market share on their competitors.

Why growth stocks?

In all my years in the business and knowing thousands of investors, I have never known a non-professional who produced really outstanding results using the value method. I know there have to be a few people out there; I've just never met them. However, I do know dozens of outstanding growth investors who have averaged 25% to 50% or more a year.

Now a money manager for William O'Neil + Co., Lee Freestone, was up 271% in 1998 and up over 100% for the first half of 1999. In 1991 at the age of 25, he entered the U.S. Investing Championship with his own personal account (real money, not play money) and was up 279%. Of course, results like this come from dedicated people who really work at it to get their exceptional returns. But it's nice to know what is possible if you are willing to spend the time and really work at it.

While it's easy to cite isolated examples of value success, most people are not Warren Buffett. People do not have his resources to thoroughly dissect a company's financial condition and properly evaluate a company's business franchise.

What about mutual funds?

If you are a mutual fund investor, you can buy either a growth fund or a value fund.

In the long run, as far as funds are concerned, it won't make much difference because the performance records are about the same. I've analyzed funds for over thirty years and have found this to be true.

The value folks claim better performance based on the value record since January 1973. It looks better because value funds are less volatile and go down less in a bear market. By beginning such a comparison at the start of the bear market in 1973–1974, value funds would naturally look better. However, if you start the same comparison at the beginning of the bull market, say in 1975, growth funds outperform value funds. Growth funds do better in up markets.

Some people prefer to own both a growth fund and a value fund in order to feel more secure. Actually, I believe quality growth funds have performed slightly better. It may be just as important to decide between a large-cap growth fund (which owns big companies) and a small-cap growth fund (whose stocks are less seasoned, more volatile and entail greater risk).

The real key is to own a sound domestic growth stock fund (not an industry or international fund). You should keep it forever. The real money in funds is made through compounding—letting the money build on itself—not by jumping in and out of funds trying to time market conditions.

SUMMARY

- There are two basic types of investors: growth stock investors and value investors.

- Growth investors seek companies with strong earnings and sales growth, superior profit margins, and a return on equity over 17%.

- Value investors search for stocks that are undervalued and have low P/E ratios.

- Our studies have shown that the new market leaders had P/Es that significantly exceeded the rest of the market (31 times the average) before they made their big advance.

- Mutual funds are a great investment as well. Pick strong performing funds from *Investor's Business Daily*'s "Mutual Funds" page, and remember the key to success with mutuals is to buy and hold forever.

LESSON 18

Don't Try to Be a Jack-Of-All-Trades

Many investors try to "get rich quick" and invest in many different, very speculative investments. In this lesson, Bill O'Neil discusses why it is best to stick with one sound investment strategy and how you can maximize your investment returns by doing so.

Why limit yourself to just good quality U.S. stocks? Plenty of other markets and investments seem to make some impressive moves.

When you first start investing, you hear about all types of intriguing opportunities to make huge profits. The list of booby traps includes foreign stocks, closed-end funds, low-priced stocks, penny stocks, options, futures, gold, convertible bonds, junk bonds, tax-free securities, and real estate partnerships. There's also watching the stock ticker tape and listening for tips from the latest guest guru appearing on the daily TV stock market shows.

My personal rule is: Always keep investing simple, basic and easy to understand. Don't try to be a jack-of-all-trades. No one can be highly successful speculating in penny Canadian mining issues, *and* buying options, *and* trading in futures *and* maneuvering in foreign stocks. The keys to success in investing—and in life—are concentration and focus. Greater risk of loss is the primary reason why new or relatively inexperienced investors should avoid most of the items mentioned above. Keep it simple.

The U.S. has the greatest stock market in the world. There are more than 10,000 U.S. common stocks to choose from. If you can't learn how to profit investing in U.S. stocks, you aren't likely to profit in the commodity market or by buying foreign stocks.

How much do you really know about a foreign government's political and economic policies, the soundness of its currency or its accounting practices? Fools often rush in where wise people fear to tread.

Many countries have a history of instability. Bernard Baruch, a well-known Wall Street speculator of years past, lost money investing in Mexico. Many of these same investment risks are still present in Mexico and South American countries.

Russia and China always seem about to emerge as the next big capitalist expansion. Yet their unsound or less-dependable government systems create enormous additional risks for investors. And, of course, there exist varying levels of corruption in some foreign governments that many U.S. investors may not be aware of. I have always recommended avoiding foreign securities. Most individual investors simply do not know all they need to know about foreign countries.

The risk associated with closed-end funds is that they often fall to a discount after the initial public offering and trade below their underlying value. Since their price is determined solely by supply and demand in the auction marketplace, there is no guarantee they will eventually sell at the price of their asset value. The discount will probably remain for years.

Why not buy low-priced stocks?

Low-priced stocks—those selling for less than $15 a share—are usually cheap for a good reason. While it may be tempting to buy a lot of shares at a low price, the financial performance of most of these issues has been poor and lags most other stocks in the market.

Do you want to put your hard-earned money into low-quality companies with deficient histories? Most institutional investors will not buy these types of stocks. Low-priced stocks are often thinly traded and simply do not have the number of shares available in the marketplace to accommodate a big institution's need to make large dollar purchases. And, as we've discussed in this book, it's the big institutional investors that move a stock's price. The best stocks don't sell at $2, $4 or $6 a share. Fortunes have been lost in cheap stocks that have poor fundamentals.

Penny stocks, which trade for under a dollar or two, can involve fraud. In addition, the difference between the bid and ask—the prices at which you buy and sell a stock—can be excessive. Imagine a penny stock costing 5/8 to buy and 1/2 to sell. Although an eighth of a point might not seem like a big spread, the stock would have to rise 20% before you could break even.

What about options and the futures market?

Stock options give investors the right to buy or sell shares of stock for a specified price by a certain time in the future. For example, if stock XYZ now trades at $50 a share and you believe it has real potential to go up, you might buy a call. That's an option to purchase say 100 shares of XYZ, in the next six months at $55 a share. If it goes to $70 a share, you'll have a worthwhile profit on a smaller initial investment in the option.

Options are risky because investors do not only have to be right about the direction of the stock but also about the time frame in which they believe the price will go up or down. It's O.K. to buy stock options as long as you limit your option activity to 10% of your total investment dollars. But even then, options are more volatile and risky.

Like stock options, futures trading involves contracts or agreements to buy or sell a particular physical commodity (grains, metals, energy products) or financial futures (interest rates, foreign currencies, stock indices) at a specified price sometime in the future.

Again, as with options, futures, due to their highly speculative nature, should be attempted only by people with several years of successful investment experience. People who have the "get rich quick" bug and commit a large percentage of their available money to options or futures are asking for trouble. They can suffer huge losses due to the extreme volatility, leverage (using borrowed money) and time limits inherent in options and futures trading. The risks are substantially higher than in common stocks.

Gold, to me, is a metal that has been overpriced for many years. It pays no dividend. Its appeal is based on fear. I prefer outstanding companies or, in poor markets, money market funds.

And bonds?

Convertible bonds, which can be exchanged for stock, are less liquid and can expose you to greater risk if you borrow heavily against them.

As far as junk bonds go, they're just that—the lowest-quality, riskiest bonds available. Because bonds are priced in relation to interest rates, you must ask yourself: How much training and experience do I have in buying bonds and assessing interest rates in the first place?

How about tax considerations?

You should make the best investment decision first rather than place your first emphasis on taxes. I've seen people become so enamored with saving tax dollars that they get into a tax saving investment that has poor returns.

If you don't have the time to devote to buying and selling the best common stocks, I would suggest a diversified domestic growth stock fund and holding it for the long term. (We will discuss investing in mutual funds later in this book.)

I know some people will disagree with my observations, but I do not like to take extra or unnecessary risks. Common stocks can be risky enough, and I can limit my risk in them by carefully selecting the better performers and having the discipline to always follow a set of sound selling rules. (We will address selling rules in Lessons 20 and 21 of this book.)

What's wrong with selecting good-quality common stocks that are #1 in their particular fields in sales and earnings growth in the last three years, and also have superior profit margins and higher ROE? You can pick stocks selling from $15 to $150 a share that are in strong industry groups and have good institutional sponsorship. The company should also have an excellent product or service, and its shares should be performing well.

The U.S. really is the best place to invest as long as you don't get the gambler's fever and try to get rich too fast. The keys to success: homework, concentration and dedication. You can do it!

SUMMARY

- When starting to invest, keep it simple. Only invest in domestic stocks or mutual funds. The more types of investments you own, the harder they are to keep track of.

- You get what you pay for in the market. Low-priced stocks are usually cheap for a good reason.

- Options are risky because investors do not only have to be right about the direction of the stock but also about the time frame in which they believe the price will go up or down.

- Futures, due to their highly speculative nature, should be attempted only by people with several years of successful investment experience.

LESSON 19

What's the Right Mix for Your Portfolio?

In this lesson, Bill O'Neil discusses how to achieve the portfolio focus you need to produce big gains.

How should you spread your risk among different stocks?

Most people in the investment business will tell you to widely diversify and to asset allocate—that is, spread your money among many types of investments in varying percentages. But you should go against this conventional wisdom, even if it makes you a little uncomfortable at first. Copying what everybody is saying and doing in the stock market may feel reassuring, but it will not be the most rewarding.

Your goal is not just to be right in the market but to make substantial money when you are right. This is best done by concentrating your eggs in fewer baskets, knowing them well and watching them carefully.

Aren't there any merits to asset allocation?

I believe in asset allocation—simple, basic allocation. Put part of your money in the best common stocks available and part in money market funds when stocks are not doing so well.

Too much diversification or allocation can lead to lack of knowledge and focus about your investments. If someone says you should have 45% in stocks, 30% in bonds, 10% in foreign stocks, 10% in money market funds and 5% in gold, this to me is misallocation. While it might be safer, it will likely reduce your overall percentage return. Maybe you shouldn't be in any bonds, foreign stocks or gold because they will hold back your total return. Fortunes were lost in bonds during the depression. And bonds are also a relatively poor inflation hedge.

So how many stocks should you own?

After setting aside whatever cash reserve you want for future emergencies, if you have $5,000 or less to invest, you should own no more than two stocks. If you have $10,000, two or three stocks is appropriate; with $25,000, perhaps three to four stocks; with $50,000, four to five; and with $100,000, you should own five to six.

There is no reason to own twenty or more stocks. You simply cannot know all you need to know about that many stocks, and it is not necessary in order to achieve great success.

What if you see other stocks you like?

At the outset, you need to decide how many stocks you'll own—and then do not exceed that limit. If your limit is six stocks, and you own six, don't buy a seventh, eighth or ninth stock, even though the temptation is there.

If a new stock is so great, force yourself to sell the least attractive of your six stocks to get money for the new name. You'll earn more by following this kind of discipline.

Is there a right way to build a concentrated portfolio?

Let's make this simple to follow: If you were to invest $100,000 in five stocks, that would be $20,000 in each stock. You aren't trying to buy a certain number of shares of a stock, but rather, a specific and similar dollar amount each time.

But stagger your buying over time. Never buy all five stocks at once. Take it one step at a time, and let your stocks prove themselves by showing at least some progress before you get 100% invested.

Is there a strategy to buying individual stocks?

Buy only half of your $20,000 position ($10,000) in one stock as your initial buy. If the stock goes down in price, don't buy any more. If it goes down 8% from your buy price, sell all of the stock at once to cut your loss.

But if the stock moves up 2% or 3% in price from your initial buy point, and if it still looks like it's acting well, you might follow up and buy $6,500 more. At this point you'd have $16,500 of your $20,000 intended position in the stock. If the stock advances 2% or 3% more, you may complete your $20,000 position by buying another $3,500. Then stop buying that stock. You've got your basic position in the stock during its first 5% advance. Sit back and give it some time and room to grow.

This concept of adding to your initial purchase in smaller quantities up to 5% from your initial buy point as the price moves up is called "pyramiding." Average up, not down. Never add money unless your prior buys seem to be working.

What else should you do when buying and managing the stocks in a portfolio?

You should use charts to help time your purchases more precisely. Don't chase stocks that are extended in price well beyond a sound base area. (See Lessons 9, 10, and 11 on base patterns.)

If your first buy falls 8% below your purchase price and you sell to cut your loss, you'll be taking a little insurance policy to protect yourself. You could easily suffer a much larger loss later if you do nothing. This 8% sell rule does not apply to stocks where you are ahead and show a large profit. At this point you can afford to be a bit more flexible.

Of course, the stocks you buy must meet all the fundamental measurements we discussed early in this book. They should be the #1 company in their field, earnings per share should be up in each of the last three years, and sales and earnings should be up a significant percentage for a number of quarters. Look for improving profit margins, return on equity of 17% or higher and a Relative Price Strength Rating of 80 or higher. The stock should be in a leading industry group and have quality institutional sponsorship.

What should you do once you own a few stocks?

After you own three or four stocks, you must learn to carefully observe and calculate which one is making the most headway, percentage-wise. That is probably your best stock and a real market leader.

So you wait for a proper time to add again to your leader. You could add perhaps the first time the stock pulls back to the fifty-day moving average line of its price. (Moving average lines on a chart smooth out the choppy daily or weekly trading activity and give you a clearer indication of the price trend.) Or you could add to your position if the stock forms a whole new base of seven or eight weeks or more and is about to break out of this new "second stage" base.

What I'm saying here is that the way to manage your portfolio effectively is to learn to recognize which stocks are actually performing best. Then try to have more of your money in those stocks and have a little less in the ones that don't act as well. You also want to have more (perhaps up to 75%) of your money in the top five or six sectors on *Investor's Business Daily*'s "52-Week Highs & Lows" feature ("New Highs" list).

As your skill at selecting top-quality market leaders improves, the day will come when you'll land upon the next Microsoft. You'll know how to have more money invested in it and make it your #1 position.

It is even more crucial to buy leading growth stocks if you are investing on margin or if you pyramid. You absolutely must realize your risk is materially increased and that you have to apply your selling rules in order to protect yourself when things go bad. But if you pyramid up, you never want to get excited and carried away and buy more shares at a higher price than you bought on your first or second purchase. This raises your average cost too high, and you will become vulnerable in the next sharp sell-off.

Once you find those real leaders, what's next?

To manage a portfolio right, you need a set of buying rules and a set of selling rules. It's one thing to buy a market leader. But it's a whole other issue to know exactly how to hang on to it, add to it at the right time, and finally sell it and get out when the stock is topping and ready for a long slide downhill.

Under this method, you might own your better-performing stocks for a year or two. The lesser ones will be sold off sooner when they show signs of not working or starting to lag substantially.

You aren't going to be right on all of your selections, and you don't have to be. But when you make a mistake, you need to always recognize it, own up to it and act. And when you have a big market leader, you need to know how to handle it so you capitalize on the stock properly and avoid shakeouts.

But isn't stock selection the hard part?

Many people have owned a Microsoft, Cisco Systems or Home Depot in the past but were shaken out on some bad news or in a general market correction. To avoid this, you should develop rules on how to properly handle a true leader once you finally find it.

In addition to this book, if you want to brush up on the rules for when to hold and when to sell, you may want to read Chapter 10 in *How to Make Money in Stocks*. This whole process of investing correctly is really a matter of reading as well as studying and learning from your actual market decisions. You can always get better and smarter.

SUMMARY

- Wide diversification and asset allocation are not necessary. Concentrate your eggs in fewer baskets, know them well and watch them carefully.

- If you have less than $5,000 to invest, only own one or two stocks. If you have $10,000—two or three stocks; $25,000—three to four stocks; $50,000—four to five stocks; and, $100,000 or more—own no more than six stocks.

- If you already own the maximum number of stocks but want to add a new stock to your portfolio, force yourself to sell the least profitable stock to get money for the new name.

- When purchasing a stock, only buy half of your desired position at the initial buy point. Buy a small amount more if the price rises 2% or 3% above your first buy. Average up in price, never down.

LESSON 20

Sell Rules Every Investor Should Master

Investors spend most of their time deciding what stock to buy. They spend little if any time thinking about when and under what circumstances their stock should be sold. This is a serious mistake.

Equal time must be devoted to developing a realistic set of selling rules. You can become a highly successful investor if you buy stocks well and sell them well. No professional athletic team would dream of having a great offense and no defense whatsoever. In this lesson, Bill O'Neil explains some of his most important sell rules.

What's the most important sell rule that investors should know?

Rule #1, of course, is to cut short your losses to protect yourself against the possibility of much greater losses. I use 8% below my purchase price of the stock as the absolute limit I'm willing to lose. Overall, your average loss will actually be less because in a few instances you can recognize when a stock is not acting properly before it drops 8% below your cost. (In Lesson 21, I will go into how to identify when a new selection may show signs of a problem and warrant a sell before you lose money.)

Here's another lesson I learned. Once my stock goes up in price a reasonable amount, I will seldom let myself lose money on the stock. Let's say my cost is $50 per share and the stock runs up to $58 or $59. If, by some chance, it comes all the way back down to $50 1/2 and I didn't take my profit when I had it, I'm certainly not going to let myself make a second mistake and wind up losing on something I had a worthwhile gain on. I'll usually sell it at that point to avoid a loss.

The greatest selling rule of all, however, is to use charts and always buy a true fundamental market leader at precisely the right time in the first place. If you always start your buying at exactly the right "pivot point" off of a sound and proper chart base, you will rarely ever take an 8% loss. In fact, you'll frequently be a few points ahead fairly quickly, and it's always helpful to get a little cushion when you start.

How do you avoid getting shaken out of a potentially outstanding stock?

About 40% of stocks you buy will pull back near your initial buy point ("pivot point")—sometimes on big volume—for one or two days. Don't get scared out on this normal yet sharp pullback in price. As long as your loss-cutting point has not been reached (8% below cost), sit tight and be patient. Sometimes it takes a number of weeks for a stock to slowly take off from its launching pad. Big money can only be made by waiting.

At other times, your stock may pull back in price to, or slightly below, its fifty-day moving average line for a day or two. This is normally a potential buying opportunity, so don't let yourself get faked out and sell at this time either.

Additionally, don't ever sell and take a profit if your leading stock runs up 20% or more in only two or three weeks. If you're really investing in a high-quality leader, rather than a low-quality, cheaper stock, the fact that your stock is up 20% or more in a short time span is an indication of its real power and potential leadership.

You must be patient and give your stock more time. Big price advances always take time to develop, so allow it at least eight or ten weeks from your first buy, then look at it again. In some cases, the stock could be up 40% or more by then.

From this point on, your stock is finally well off the launching pad, and you now can wait for it to trigger any one of a number of different sell rules to take a significant profit in your stock while it's on the way up in price. You want to learn to sell while it's still advancing.

What are some of those sell rules?

About 30% of market leaders will peak after many months of advance by having what is called a "climax top." The stock will run up at a much faster rate than in prior weeks, usually 25% to 50% in one to three weeks. It could be up in price eight out of ten days and daily trading volume generally picks up.

One of the days towards the end will probably show the stock's greatest one-day price advance since the beginning of the move up. Sell into this unusually strong price action. Because of your selection criteria, you probably bought when most people were hesitant and unsure. Now you sell when everyone's excited and bubbling over about how terrific the stock is. Successful decisions in the stock market often are contrary to mass opinion.

You might also consider selling when a stock's P/E ratio increases 130% or more from the time the stock originally began its big move out of its initial base pattern.

Some of your stocks may be sold when the stock's price goes through its upper channel line by 2% or 3%. The upper and lower channel lines of a stock are determined by drawing a straight line connecting three of the price high peaks and a second parallel line connecting three price lows during the same period.

These parallel lines should be drawn using the overall, long-term uptrend. Channel lines drawn over too short a time period can be premature, so make sure the three peak points you pick cover a number of months.

Most market leaders could last for a year or more. So if you get nervous or influenced by news or other people's opinions and sell to take your profit in only the fourth, fifth or sixth week of a stock's advance, you'll likely be too early. Eventually, you'll sell out of a giant winner that roars on substantially higher, and you'll be kicking yourself.

I encourage you to go back and review Lesson 13 of this book, which illustrates how to recognize the beginning of a general market top. This can be a signal to sell and cut back a stock or two. In the next lesson, we'll cover more rules on recognizing activity in your stock that will alert you when to sell and take a profit. Through simple rules, you can learn to be a good seller as well as a good buyer.

SUMMARY

- The #1 rule is to cut your losses short to protect yourself against the possibility of much greater losses. If a stock falls 8% below your purchase price, sell it.

- Don't sell and take a profit if your market leading stock is up *20% to 25%* in only two or three weeks. That's a sign of real power, and you may be holding a big winner.

- Don't let yourself lose money on a stock you had a reasonable profit in.

- 40% of stocks will pull back near the initial buy point—sometimes on big volume—for one or two days. Don't let this shake you out of your stock.

- 30% of market leaders will peak after many months of advance by having what is called a "climax top." The stock will run up at a much faster rate than in prior weeks. Look for the stock's greatest one-day price advance since the beginning of the move up. This usually means that everyone is excited about the stock which makes its price rise dramatically. Because the market often moves contrary to mass opinion, it is a good idea to sell your stock when this happens.

More Sell Rules Every Investor Should Master

In this lesson, Bill O'Neil continues his discussion of the most important selling rules.

What advice do you have for someone who wants to start investing today?

Everyone can and should learn to invest in the U.S., the leading economic power in the world. By reading this book, you should have the proper foundation and rules to be a successful investor. With that in hand, it's then a matter of gaining knowledge, skill, experience and discipline by actually getting in and doing it.

You will always get better as long as you're willing to do a post-evaluation of all your decisions to learn from your inevitable mistakes. Never let yourself get discouraged by temporary setbacks. It is definitely possible to make 50% to 100% or even more in nearly every good market year once you gain the skills to know when and what to buy and when to sell. You may want to consider re-reading this book several times to remind yourself of the rules.

What other selling rules do you have?

Here are some additional selling rules to help you nail down big profits:

1. If the earnings per share of a stock show a major deceleration in growth for two consecutive quarters, the stock should probably be sold (i.e., if earnings have been up 100% for a number of quarters and then slow down to say 30% and then 20%).

2. If your stock breaks out of a chart base and the daily or weekly trading volume is less on the day or week it breaks out than the prior day or week, it is showing poor demand at a key point and the stock should, in most cases, be sold. Volume should be up 40% to 50% or more than its average daily volume.

3. If a stock breaks out of a base pattern on substantial volume one day but immediately fails to "follow-through" and then goes down in price on increased volume for several days, to the point where it may be 4% or 5% below the breakout or "pivot point," it could indicate a faulty price pattern. The stock, in most cases, should be cut back or sold. Don't be discouraged—you can't expect to be right every time.

4. If your stock has advanced a significant distance over many months and has formed several bases during the process, the fourth time the stock breaks out of a base, it should probably be sold. By this time, the stock is on everyone's radar screen, and the obvious rarely works in the stock market.

5. If the real market leaders in a particular industry break down in price, are being sold in volume and are unable to regain much ground, then most of the others in the group will probably be vulnerable and should be considered for selling.

6. After your stock has had an extended price advance over more than just one or two months and its price opens up on a gap from the prior day's high, the stock should probably be sold. It usually indicates the last "stage" of its move. This is termed an exhaustion gap. However, gaps that occur closer in time and distance to a sound base pattern are not normally a problem, so be sure not to confuse exhaustion gaps with gaps that occur in the early stages of a breakaway move.

7. Sometimes if a stock closes down in price on the largest one-day volume since the beginning of its long price advance over many months, it could be a warning sign for you to consider selling.

8. Sometimes I'll sell a stock with a profit because it moves up in price less than another stock I'm holding. The money in it can be used in the better performing stock.

Once in the last half of 1990, I sold a position in Home Depot, an excellent company that I bought at just the right time, and one I was certain was going to double in price. I wanted to buy more Amgen with the money. It was acting relatively stronger, had bigger earnings projections, and the potential to triple in price. This is a rare move, but it illustrates how you must learn over a period of time to sense which of your stocks is your real market leader.

What is the best way to improve your ability to sell stocks? Get into the habit of doing an analysis every year of all your buy and sell decisions. Get a chart service and plot where you bought and sold each of your stocks.

Separate your decisions that were profitable from the ones that didn't work out so well. Spend a few weeks studying the two groups. Do you see a common thread in the ones that worked? Do you see consistent problems in the ones that didn't?

I guarantee you'll make some valuable discoveries that will lead to your creating a new rule or two to correct certain mistakes you may have repeated. Be objective. Be willing to look at your mistakes.

Most people will not take the time to study and analyze what they are doing right and what they are doing wrong. But this is how you improve and get to be really good at what you're doing—in the market and in life. Personal opinions, pride, ego, and the desire to save face and prove you're right have absolutely no place in the stock market and will cost you dearly—so you'd better learn to objectively analyze your mistakes. It's never too late to learn.

SUMMARY

- Sell a stock if the earnings per share shows a major deceleration in growth for two quarters in a row.

- If your stock advances a significant distance over many months and has formed several bases during the process, the fourth time the stock breaks out of a base ("fourth stage" base), it probably should be sold.

- Sometimes, you should sell a stock because it consistently moves up in price less than another good stock you're holding. The money can be used in the better performing stock. Review the selling rules in this lesson and Lesson 20 on a regular basis. Learn them and commit them to memory.

How to Make a Million with Mutuals

Investor's Business Daily's *founder and chairman, Bill O'Neil, has a distinctly different outlook on mutual funds compared to his views on individual stocks.*

What do you think of mutual funds?

Mutual funds are the best investment medium ever produced for many individual investors. They are easy to use and widely accessible for individual sale, as well as through corporate and government retirement programs.

One reason for their popularity is their relatively low cost. By pooling the assets of many people, funds achieve economies of scale that cut their cost of investing while generating substantial long-term returns for their investors.

A diversified U.S. stock fund is always the first-class way to go, in my view. I don't want bond funds, income funds, balanced funds, industry funds or foreign funds. You simply can't know all you need to know about all different types of funds.

Also, because a majority of the real growth occurs in the companies traded on the U.S. exchanges, why not concentrate on funds that invest in companies you know about and are familiar with? Funds, I believe, are better, safer and more liquid investments, in most instances, than private business ventures, loans, art, coins, savings and loan accounts, trust deeds or real estate.

Which type of fund do you prefer?

A stock fund can be either a value fund, investing in stocks deemed to be undervalued in price or a growth stock fund that focuses on companies with expanding profits. A fund might also specialize in either large-capitalization stocks or smaller companies. A fund also could be smaller or larger in terms of assets under management.

In any case, you should stick to proven, basic formats. Keep it simple. You don't need the latest fad in funds, whether it be micro-cap funds, funds of funds, or some new closed-end fund.

The fund you opt for doesn't have to be the absolute hottest performer for the year. You should do well if you check out an A+ or A rated fund in *Investor's Business Daily*'s "Mutual Fund" tables. *Investor's Business Daily*'s three-year performance rating grades all funds on a scale from A+ (representing the top 5% of performers) to E (the laggard performers). You also should probably avoid the fastest moving, most volatile fund because it will be invested in lower-quality, less-proven stocks trading with much less volume. These stocks will not be as marketable when the fund grows in size or faces bear-market declines.

When should you sell a mutual fund?

There's only one real secret to success when you acquire a mutual fund. It's something not everyone understands or has the patience to implement. It's easy: You never, ever sell a domestic, diversified growth stock mutual fund. You hold it until you die, so to speak.

Here's why: A 200-year logarithmic chart of the U.S. stock market averages proves that the U.S. market has continually grown as our population, economy and standard of living has continually increased. I have included a logarithmic chart on the next page for you to see.

This natural rate of growth actually accelerated after we were victorious in World War II. We've come through wars, recessions, depressions—you name it. Our system of freedom and opportunity has proven to be the most successful in the world. Invention and innovation continue to drive our unparalleled advances. Many people, out of fear or lack of information, constantly underestimate the depth and strength of the U.S. system, its people and its economy.

As with everything, you can expect to have some down years with your mutual fund investments. However, this is really irrelevant, because a professionally managed diversified portfolio will in time recover and rebound along with the economy.

A wisely selected fund could possibly double in value every five or six years because of the principle of compounding. Compounding involves constantly allowing greater sums of money to work for you.

If you begin with $5,000, you could have $10,000 at the end of your first five or six years. Your next five or six-year period would see your $10,000 mutual fund portfolio shoot up by, not another $5,000, but by $10,000. And the following period could see your $20,000 swell to $40,000, and then $80,000, and so on.

The key here is the magic of compounding. That's why I say never sell a good U.S. growth stock fund. The compounding will make you

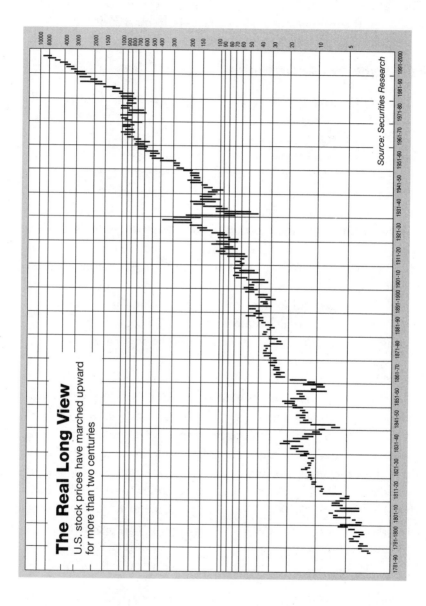

The Real Long View

U.S. stock prices have marched upward
for more than two centuries

Source: Securities Research

a mind-boggling fortune if you simply have the sense to make your fund a permanent investment. Sit tight and stop worrying. Go out and enjoy life.

If you play out the scenario for a few more cycles, your $80,000 would be $160,000, and the $160,000 could mushroom to $320,000, and this is assuming you only forked over an initial $5,000! You would make even more if you added money every month or every year, plus added extra to your fund during each bear market sell-off. Today, it's possible for anyone in America to become a millionaire by investing in mutual funds.

And you don't have to sell when you reach 65 or 70 years of age, either. If you need income, just set up a monthly or quarterly withdrawal plan to take out 7% or 8% each year.

Should you diversify your fund holdings?

As time goes along, it's O.K. to buy a second or third fund. You might want both a growth fund and a value fund or perhaps an index fund. However, you don't need to diversify among eight or ten funds because, in most cases, it will serve to water down your total return by 3% or 4% per year. Overdiversifying with too many funds can be counterproductive.

Most mutual fund companies have a big fund family of twenty to fifty funds or more. That's so they've got something for every season (bull or bear market) and every demand in the marketplace. Because there are so many fund options available, it's natural then that asset allocation, the practice of allocating a certain percentage of your portfolio to varying types of investments or funds, has become popular.

However, I'm not a big advocate of allocation programs because, while they may provide a hint of added safety, they will almost always reduce your overall annual returns. And it might cost you more if wide diversification forces you into higher commission brackets in the case of funds with sales charges.

Also, along with allocation comes the recommended switching to more of a certain category and less of another. These switches have not improved performance over time. My guess is that you will blow another percent or two a year on all of this messing around. Why? Because historically most industry officials aren't truly experts at forecasting market tops and bottoms or trend shifts.

Also, I wouldn't agonize over whether the fund's management fee is low or high, or whether its portfolio turnover rate and commissions are low or high. A strong net performance record is the bottom line, regardless of fees or trading activity. If you were going to have a heart operation, would you search for and go with the physician quoting the cheapest fee?

And I also wouldn't switch out of a fund just because it has grown large in size. Perhaps size could turn out to be an advantage in the age of investing in larger capitalization stocks. Those people who still own Fidelity Magellan or Janus Fund are still compounding their profits, and both were up more than the S&P 500 during the late 1990s.

SUMMARY

- A diversified U.S. stock fund, whether growth or value, is your best choice.

- Choose funds with an A or A+ rating from *Investor's Business Daily*. They are the best performers over a 36-month period.

- Never sell a domestic growth stock mutual fund. Hold it and watch its growth compound over the years ahead.

- Don't buy too many funds. Extensive asset allocation will just dilute your overall returns.

- Compounding over the long-term is the key to making a million in mutual funds.

LESSON 23

Too Busy? How to Use Investor's Business Daily in Twenty Minutes

If you're a busy executive, professional or individual investor trying to keep up in this age of information overload . . . keep reading. The following lesson could prove to be invaluable.

Investor's Business Daily *was specifically designed to efficiently present all the important news of the day and cut down dramatically on the time it takes to research profitable investment decisions. Here's how to read* Investor's Business Daily *in only twenty to thirty minutes a day.*

What sections do you recommend investors read for news and quick updates?

Quickly scan "IBD's Top 10" news stories in the first two columns on the front page and "The Markets" short summary box in the third column. Read the short items you're interested in. Then quickly scan the headlines on page A2's "To the Point" and read only the brief summaries you find important.

Investor's Business Daily's first two pages are categorized and organized into short "briefs" designed to give you all of the day's key news items while saving you valuable time. Few people today have time to read two or three newspapers and watch the TV news.

If you're an executive or just interested in advancing your career, you may want to spend more time with the first several pages of *Investor's Business Daily*. Glance at the headlines for these features:

- **The New America,** to stay up on dynamic entrepreneurial companies with new ideas, new concepts and new products. These could be the new market leaders.

- **Leaders & Success,** to gain crucial knowledge from world-class leaders and the most successful people from all fields. You'll gain practical insights that can help to further your success.

- **Business & the Economy,** along with Leaders & Success, is a must read for anyone in management.

- **Computers & Technology,** concentrates on high-tech issues and products and is written by experienced journalists in our Silicon Valley bureau. Note any stories you want to read later when you have more time available.

Where should readers look for market information?

Before delving into the unique stock market information contained in *Investor's Business Daily's* pages, it's important to give you a context for how this information was developed.

Following years of research of the most successful stocks since 1953, *Investor's Business Daily's* sister company developed the first U.S. historical stock database. Today, it tracks over 3,000 data items on nearly

10,000 publicly traded companies, as well as 9,600 mutual funds. This database is used by the majority of the largest institutional investors (mutual funds, banks, etc.) to help them screen for future winners.

Investor's Business Daily is really a daily computer print out and evaluation of the entire market. It provides relative scores, ratings and special screens, based on extensive stock market research, of the most relevant factors in winning stocks. Items proven to be significantly less relevant in these same research studies were omitted from the paper. This is the reason why dividends, P/Es, etc. are given less space in *Investor's Business Daily*'s stock tables.

How do you identify potential market leaders in Investor's Business Daily?

Investor's Business Daily's unique stock tables do 80% of your research work for you and in a lot less time. I suggest you read and learn to understand the simple stock ratings explained in the "How to Use IBD SmartSelect™ Corporate Ratings" box located at the top of the NYSE tables page.

Most people merely use stock tables to check the prices of stocks they own. They're often unaware of and have not yet learned to capitalize on the powerful proprietary information *Investor's Business Daily*'s tables contain. *Investor's Business Daily* is not like the business section of your local paper or *The Wall Street Journal*. It is an extensive research tool with vital analysis and ratings designed to help you identify outstanding new investment ideas. Always grab a pen so you can note any stocks you want to investigate further.

With all that in mind, how do I use *Investor's Business Daily* to find superior new ideas and to get a solid feel for what's going on in the market?

The first place I turn to is "Where the Big Money's Flowing" at the beginning of the NYSE and Nasdaq tables. These lists highlight stocks that have the greatest increase in trading volume above their normal trading levels (indicating large professional buying or selling). I look at the company names of those up in price, then quickly scan the boldfaced names. I then go through the NYSE and Nasdaq tables, from A to Z, only scanning the companies shown in boldfaced type.

Investor's Business Daily boldfaces those stocks that are up $1 or more for the day and those hitting a new price high (a sign of strength). I circle some of the boldfaced stocks with high IBD *SmartSelect™* Corporate Ratings. These are stocks I am usually familiar with and may want to check out further for possible new investments.

Next, I scan the company names on the "Best Ups" list in "Earnings News." This section highlights companies showing the biggest increases in quarterly earnings just reported.

In addition to the stock listings, special screens, and individual "mini-charts" presented in *Investor's Business Daily*, the Mutual Fund section is another great place to identify potential new market leaders that are getting the attention of top mutual fund managers.

Specifically, I check the "10 Largest U.S. Holdings," the "Top Sells," and particularly the top two or three stocks on the "Top New Buys" list of the two or three mutual funds that have performed strongly for the year. This information is displayed in the Mutual Fund profiles on the "Making Money in Mutuals" page.

IBD *SmartSelect™* **CORPORATE RATINGS**
┌ Earnings Per Share
  ┌ Relative Price Strength
    ┌ Industry Group Relative Strength
      ┌ Sales+Profit Margins+ROE
        ┌ Accumulation/Distribution

52 Wk High	Stock	Symbol	Closing Price	Price Chg	Vol% Chg	Vol 100s	Spon. Rank	Day's High	Low	
96 37 E BD 19	AmerOnclgy	AORI	10	+ 1/2	+32	3239	18	10 1/2	9 5/8	o
75 71 C DB 11 5/8	AmerPacfc cr	APFC	8 9/32	+ 1/32	-89	32	23	8 9/32	8 7/32	
90 96 B AB 37 11/16	**AmerPwCon**	**APCC**	36 5/8	+1 1/8	+72	1.4m	26	36 15/16	33 3/8	o
63 41 B AB 15 1/16	AmerSfins	AMSFF	9	- 1/2	-88	19	9	9 1/8	9	k
34 23 D BC 23 1/4	AmerSaRazr	RAZR	9 9/16	+	-89	83	9	10	9 1/2	o
57 9 B BE 36 3/4	Amerilink	ALNK	8	- 3/8	-58	134	9	8 3/8	8	-
96 41 B AE 33 7/8	Amerin	AMRN	21 3/16	- 1/16	-43	774	12	21 3/4	20 7/8	o
97 49 A AB 20 1/4	AmeriPath	PATH	12 1/8	+ 3/4	-45	666	17	12 3/16	11 1/4	o
81 96 C AB 79 3/8	**Amgen**	r5 **AMGN**	73 1/4	+1 5/8	-11	2.7m	26	73 5/8	71 5/8	o
42 97 C AB 26 12/16	AmeriTrade	AMTD	18 7/16	+ 3/16	-73	997	99	18 3/16	17 13/16	o
80 98 A AB 48 1/8	*ArterialVasc* c	AVEI	44 1/8	- 7/8	-54	7374	25	45 1/8	43 5/8	o

Generally only one out of every fifteen or twenty bolded stocks also has outstanding IBD *SmartSelect*™ Corporate Ratings and is sponsored by the better funds. In time, you will more easily recognize the bolded stocks that mutual funds have shown interest in and whose charts are showing signs of sound price bases or other indications of accumulation (professional buying). After this highly selective filtering process, you should have just a handful of top-rated stocks noted for further analysis and possible purchase.

Access to a chart service can save you further research time and, as you learn more, will improve the selection and timing of your investments.

How do you gauge market and industry trends?

I strongly suggest you read "The Big Picture" on the "General Market & Sectors" page every day. It will give you a professional summary of the important happenings in the market with a step-by-step, numbered analysis pointing to key indicators on the accompanying charts. I also check the Nasdaq, S&P 500 and Dow index daily price and volume charts and the percent change for the day.

Next, you should always observe the first five industry groups with the most stocks making new price highs in *Investor's Business Daily's* "52-Week Highs & Lows" feature ("New Highs" list) shown on the accompanying "Industry Groups" page. This is an excellent place to identify the leading industries in the market at any time. A final quick peek at the small chart of "Big-Cap Growth Funds vs. Small-Cap Growth Funds" will tell you if larger or smaller stocks have been leading the market. This helps you concentrate your portfolio in the type of securities that are in large demand.

Investor's Business Daily is more than just a newspaper. It's a superior *research tool* based on proven historical models that helps you efficiently zero in on the best companies in the best industries. Spending only twenty to thirty minutes each day with *Investor's Business Daily* could put you on the road to investment success.

SUMMARY

- *Investor's Business Daily* was designed to help save you time and give you all of the important news of the day.

- Features such as "The New America," "Computers & Technology" and "Investor's Corner" are filled with new investment ideas.

- *Investor's Business Daily*'s unique stock tables can help you pick potential stock market leaders. These tables include proprietary analytical data that are easy to read and use.

- Before selecting your stocks, you must be able to gauge the general market. "The Big Picture" on the "General Market & Sectors" page will show you what is going on in the market now.

How to Make the Most of Investor's Business Daily, Investors.com, and Other Online Resources

Independent research from Intelliquest compared Investor's Business Daily *to* The Wall Street Journal, Fortune, Forbes, Business Week *and* Barron's *and ranked* Investor's Business Daily #1 *in readers who are high-end computer users and buyers.* Investor's Business Daily's *readers are computer-savvy, and many use the paper in conjunction with online resources in order to cut down on the time it takes to identify and then research potential investments.*

How do you view the web as a research medium?

There isn't much that you can't find on the web these days. The problem is no longer too little information but rather information overload that has all of our heads spinning.

The web has two distinct faces. If you know exactly what you're looking for and exactly where to find it, the internet is convenient and can save you time. If, on the other hand, you are searching for ideas and attempting to evaluate massive amounts of data, you could easily get lost and overwhelmed in cyberspace.

Can you use Investor's Business Daily and the internet together?

I see *Investor's Business Daily* and the internet as powerful tools to use in combination. The internet can lead you to everything from company financial statements and stock charts to promoters hyping the latest thing. But amid all this noise, do you have the time and the expertise to evaluate all the information available? Do you know whom to trust? Where is the information coming from? Do you have a highly accurate sense of the relative importance among all these puzzle pieces?

Investor's Business Daily is about clarity—and true relevance. Think of *Investor's Business Daily* as your filtering system. It provides special screens to zero in on the potential leaders from a universe of over 10,000 stocks. *Investor's Business Daily* taps into (what's considered to be) the most comprehensive and expansive database on stocks available today.

It's the same database that more than 400 of the largest institutions such as Fidelity Fund, JP Morgan and Putnam use for research. This is the only database in the country derived from years of research into the specific criteria of the most successful stocks.

Investor's Business Daily is designed to do most of your homework for you. How much would it cost you to track 10,000 stocks and maintain a daily spreadsheet and compare hundreds of variables per company to determine their relative investment potential? And how much is your time worth? Navigating the web, picking up bits and pieces from different sites, simply does not give you the whole picture.

Do you see any problems with the internet?

There is a false sense of security on the internet. Because of the overwhelming amounts of information available at your fingertips, most people do not consider the potential bias of the information providers. Whether or not they charge for their services, most groups on the internet are not there out of the kindness of their hearts. Rather, every web site is a business. While there are many sound web sites, there are also a number of providers that are actually in the stock-promotion business.

With the freedom of the relatively young internet also comes possible abuse. Many people have been burned on the internet. The Securities and Exchange Commission is investigating groups that may have taken advantage of investors over the web.

Investor's Business Daily is a national business and financial newspaper—an independent, objective provider of relevant market facts and data. With objective data comes a reduction of emotionally driven decisions. Through chat rooms and message boards there can, at times, exist an almost unhealthy level of frenzy or emotion with regard to a stock.

This sometimes encourages a herd mentality and makes it easy to make snap decisions based on hype rather than critical facts. Every day we talk to hundreds of subscribers who use the internet to generate investment ideas, but then use *Investor's Business Daily* as an objective check or validation resource.

In separating out the facts from the hype, I would encourage people to visit company web sites, the Edgar database (www.sec.gov/edgarhp .htm) for company filings and the exchange web sites (www.nasdaq, nyse and amex.com). While online, check out *Investor's Business Daily*'s web site, www.investors.com, for news, research, and educational tutorials.

For sophisticated charts and data on over seventy fundamental and technical items on over 10,000 stocks, Daily Graphs Online, a subscription-based service, taps into the same database as *Investor's Business Daily*. For a free trial, visit www.dailygraphs.com.

SUMMARY

- There is so much information available on the internet these days, it's easy to get overloaded. Use *Investor's Business Daily* to find the very best stocks before you visit the internet for further information.

- *Investor's Business Daily* can save you time by giving you the most relevant information in one place.

- Consider the potential bias of information providers over the internet.

How to Learn from Models of Success

Bill O'Neil has spent many years studying what works—in the stock market and in life. In this lesson, Bill O'Neil discusses why it's important to study models of success and reveals some of his findings.

Why is examining examples of success so important?

Investor's Business Daily would not exist today if it were not for building and studying models of the most successful stocks and investors.

Years ago, I studied models of every new stock investment made over a two-year period by the top-performing mutual fund at the time. From that analysis, I learned the key characteristics of the very best stock investments and the proper time to buy them.

Lessons learned from observing those models, plus doing an analysis of my own investment mistakes, enabled me a few years later to buy a seat on the New York Stock Exchange after starting from virtually nothing.

Since that time, we've continued to build and analyze models of every outstanding publicly traded company from 1953 through today. The information and principles gained from these models of success led to a number of successful investments, which in turn allowed us to launch *Investor's Business Daily*.

The solid foundation behind all the valuable data, charts and statistics in *Investor's Business Daily* is based on years of research, model-building and the creation of a proprietary stock market database that really works. It's also the reason why so many people have success with *Investor's Business Daily*. Once they learn how to take advantage of *Investor's Business Daily*'s unique ratings, charts and screens, they often see significant improvements in their investment results.

Does that method of studying models of the most successful stocks work just as well in identifying characteristics of truly successful people?

That's the question we asked ourselves, and we found that it does. When we first started reporting on successful people more than ten years ago, some people questioned how that fit into *Investor's Business Daily*. The truth is, people who subscribe to *Investor's Business Daily* are the same individuals who are seeking out ways to improve themselves and grow. It was simply another way of learning from what works, and learning from the most successful people.

Investor's Business Daily studied hundreds of leaders from all walks of life: business people, athletes, artists, doctors, religious and social leaders, etc. We discovered most had ten important traits in common that, when combined, made these people immensely successful.

These traits were the inspiration for our "Leaders & Success" page and "*IBD*'s 10 Secrets to Success." They are both great training tools for company managers and future leaders, even for parents raising children.

Everyone can learn, profit and be inspired by these positive stories and examples. Unlike regular biographies, *Investor's Business Daily*'s "Leaders & Success" page goes beyond what someone accomplished to explain the practical steps and actions they took. You'll see just how they reached success, along with the obstacles they had to overcome to get there.

These are things that all of us can immediately put to use to help us think differently, create new habits and aspire to even greater heights.

What are the ten traits of successful people?

Our research found the following common leadership characteristics:

1. *Positive thinking.* Almost without exception, successful people think positively. They think of success, not failure. They are able to be positive regardless of how difficult the situation, which allows them to rebound from obstacles and problems. Their attitudes determine their fates.

   Pat Riley, the NBA coach who led the Los Angeles Lakers to four titles in the 1980s, says his father taught him something he has never forgotten: "It's not what happens to you that's important—it's how you react to it." Successful people don't let negative people or environments throw them off track. Study successful people who were able to overcome real problems. Find out how they did it—how you can do it.

2. *Leaders make conscious decisions regarding what they're after, what they want.* Then they draw out specific plans to reach their goals. When Muhammad Ali was thirteen and weighed only 115 pounds, he made up his mind that his one and only goal was to be heavyweight champion of the world.

3. *Goals are nothing without action.* We found that leaders and successful individuals are very action-oriented. They are always on the move.

   Sam Walton of Wal-Mart visited Sol Price in San Diego, where he toured one of the first Price Club warehouses. That same night when Walton returned to Arkansas, he had his architects stay up all night drafting plans for the new Sam's Clubs. Decision and action can and should be instantaneous and simultaneous.

4. *Successful people never stop learning.* They read books, get extra training to acquire skills and seek out mentors.

   A fascinating discovery we made in our research was that you could almost forecast later success at an early age based on successful people doing two very specific things as children. They had many different jobs or responsibilities from the time they were in the third grade through high school, and they were all avid readers from an early age. Since most people don't read many books, readers tend to become leaders. John Wooden, who coached UCLA to ten college basketball championships said: "It's what you learn after you know it all that counts."

5. *Without a doubt, success is a result of being persistent and working hard.* Leaders treat success like a marathon, not a sprint. They don't let themselves get discouraged, and they never give up.

   The Beatles were turned down by every record company in England before their success. Michael Jordan was cut from his high school varsity basketball team. Albert Einstein made an "F" in math. John Wooden coached at UCLA for thirteen years before he won a national championship. Thomas Edison once said: "Many of life's failures are people who didn't realize how close they were to success when they gave up."

6. *Successful people learn to analyze details and seek out all the facts.* Many of these individuals can be considered perfectionists in that they went far beyond what was normal in terms of details and research. They also analyzed themselves. Successful people put ego aside to carefully learn from their mistakes in order to improve.

7. *Focusing time and money is another key characteristic of success.* Learning to save money and focusing time showed up again and again. Successful people don't let other people or things distract them from their goals. With regard to any goal, Henry Ford once said that a person "ought to think of it by day and dream of it by night."

8. *Success often means doing something differently, being innovative.* Most people who are successful find a different and better way to do things—and are often criticized in the process. The head of Western Union had an opportunity to innovate when Alexander Graham Bell offered to sell a part interest in his new telephone. The man turned it down with the comment, "What would we do with an interesting toy like that?" Sam Walton encourages others to "swim upstream, go the other way, ignore conventional wisdom. If everyone is doing it one way, there's a good chance you can find your niche by going in exactly the opposite direction."

9. *Successful people deal and communicate with others effectively.* They serve as coaches, motivators and inspiration for others. Dale Carnegie wrote the bible on this subject with *How to Win Friends and Influence People.*

10. *Long-term success comes from integrity.* Those researched were honest, dependable and took responsibility. They set an example for those around them and did not compromise their principles. Without this final trait, Numbers 1 through 9 won't matter.

Anyone can strive to become the best in the field of his or her choice. Just as you would with stocks, if you study and apply the characteristics culled from models and examples of great leaders, you too can achieve greater success.

APPENDIX B

Tales of Investors' Successes and Failures

To learn to be a better investor, you will experience success and failure in the market. This is all a part of the process. But it is important to learn from your own mistakes as well as the mistakes of others so you can grow and minimize future errors you make. In this appendix, Bill O'Neil will share successes and failures from investors he's met.

What successes and failures of individual investors stand out in your mind?

I work out at a gym and remember recently two men in their 40s approaching me and telling me that they'd attended one of our investment seminars back in the 1980s. I asked them how they had fared in their investments since then. The first one said he owned a bunch of oil stocks and was down about 20% for 1998.

I quizzed him about the reasons for his stock selections as they all showed low Relative Price Strength Ratings and Earnings Per Share Ratings. His response: "I'm a long-term investor, and I'm prepared to sit with them for several years." Rather than following a set of proven rules, this gentleman relied on personal opinions and emotions to guide his buy and sell decisions.

The other man had an interesting story. He was a CPA, a trained professional with five years of college financial and accounting courses. He proceeded to tell me how crazy he felt the market was acting, that none of it made any sense, that price/earnings ratios were ridiculous and out of line, etc.

When I asked about his success in the market, he told me he got wiped out in 1987 because he was fully margined in a $30 lower-quality stock when it took a nose dive and collapsed to $3 a share. I reminded the man that this is precisely why rule #1 is to cut losses at 8% so you don't suffer losses you can't recover from.

While he acknowledged owning all the educational tapes, books and pamphlets we've put out, he frowned and was a bit embarrassed about his failure to actually watch, read and put this information into practice.

What do ego and overconfidence do to investment decisions?

It's surprising to think that very intelligent people with high IQs can easily make the connection between years of training and schooling for their profession of choice, and yet fail to make the same connection between training and hard work when it comes to being highly successful in the stock market.

Both of these men were intelligent and otherwise reasonably successful. But a high IQ means absolutely nothing in the stock market. In fact, it may work against you because intelligence is usually coupled with ego and overconfidence. Over the years, I've come to realize that ego is deadly in the market. It's when people attempt to prove they're smarter than the market that they stop learning and close their minds to ways of doing things that are different from their comfortable habits and past patterns.

Can you give us an example of someone who has followed the rules?

Several months ago a woman in her 40s thanked me for the investment courses she had attended. She mentioned that she had better performance in the market than she ever thought possible. She bought stocks like The Gap, Intel, Cisco Systems and Microsoft by following what she'd learned to the letter: only investing in those with high EPS and Relative Price Strength Ratings, with high profit margins, that were leaders in their respective fields, etc.

Another woman approached me just before a seminar and introduced me to her two young sons. She had brought them so they could learn about investing. As the boys turned and walked away just out of earshot, the woman whispered to me that she had made more than a million dollars by just following the rules.

Then there was a young man who, over the course of the years, has attended about thirty free *Investor's Business Daily* seminars and eleven or twelve paid all-day workshops. He made 150% profit in one year and was up more than 1,000% over several years. I wondered why in the world he kept coming back, again and again, to the seminars. He told me he had to keep coming back in order to stay focused on all the critical things and not to get thrown off by all the "noise" out there.

Another older man stood up at a seminar Q&A session a few years back. He told the audience he had attended a seminar back in the mid-1980s when we mentioned Home Depot. At that point, and after doing his homework, he purchased 1,000 shares of Home Depot. This time he was back to ask me what he should do with his Home Depot. (It had only split eight times!) I told him to go buy himself a Cadillac and enjoy it.

I also met a woman who was able to finance her brother's medical school tuition with the money she made in the market.

Any other tales you'd like to share?

Meanwhile, back at the gym in the summer of 1998, I remember over-hearing two young guys talk about how overpriced Yahoo! was. I happened to own a few shares. After hearing all the disbelief and knowing the market generally disappoints the masses, I realized that Yahoo! was probably headed higher. Next, their subject switched to one of the men telling the other about the $1.50 a share stock he purchased a few days earlier.

Twice at the gym I've heard someone giving a listener this "sage" advice: "If you buy it and it goes down in price, just buy more and it will come back in price." I've learned that not all stocks that fall in price recover.

Any final thoughts?

Like the woman attending a seminar with her boys, many parents and teachers use *Investor's Business Daily* to teach children about financial empowerment and to help give them an edge in the years to come. A group of seventh-graders in Massachusetts used *Investor's Business Daily* to outperform professional money managers in a stock-picking contest.

Investor's Business Daily is not only investment training, it's life training. I am pleased by the number of letters and e-mails we get from parents who are teaching their kids to read with the "Leaders & Success" page.

And it's not just children. Recently, I received a moving letter from a young man incarcerated in a state prison. He said the "Leaders & Success" page was helping him and other inmates find new ways of thinking about life and what awaits them once they return to society.

I hope this book of lessons will help you find success in investing, in your career, and in your personal life. We appreciate all the stories we receive daily from people wanting to share their successes with us. We wish you continued success in all areas of your life. Good luck!

Recommended Reading List

- *How to Make Money in Stocks*
  William J. O'Neil
- *The Battle for Investment Survival*
  G. M. Loeb
- *Tape Reading and Market Tactics*
  H. Neil
- *How to Trade in Stocks*
  J. Livermore
- *Reminiscences of a Stock Operator*
  E. Lefevre
- *The Sophisticated Investor*
  Burton Cane
- *How I Made Two Million Dollars in the Stock Market*
  N. Darvas
- *My Own Story*
  Bernard Baruch
- *One Up on Wall Street*
  Peter Lynch
- *How to Buy Stocks (for beginners only)*
  Louis Engel
- *Investor's Business Daily*

Glossary

Acceleration (in earnings, in sales): An indicator of strength in a company. Generally speaking, acceleration represents an increase in the earnings or sales growth rate quarter over quarter. The strongest companies show a greater percentage increase in each of the last three or four quarters. For example, Company XYZ's earnings growth rate might look like this: (Q1) +20%, (Q2) +27%, (Q3) +52%, (Q4) +59%. (*Also, see* Earnings growth)

Accumulation: Buying of stock by institutional or professional investors. (*Also, see* Institutional investors)

Accumulation/Distribution Rating: Exclusive rating in *Investor's Business Daily*. One of the IBD *SmartSelect*™ Corporate Ratings, it tracks the relative degree of institutional buying (accumulation) and selling (distribution) in a particular stock over the last 13 weeks. Updated daily, stocks are rated on an A to E scale:

A = Heavy buying

B = Moderate buying

C = Equal amounts of buying and selling

D = Moderate selling

E = Heavy selling

Advance/Decline Line: The Advance/Decline Line is derived from the total number of stocks advancing versus the number declining in price each day on the New York Stock Exchange (NYSE). A technical general market and timing tool that is often misused or misinterpreted by investors.

Annual earnings: A longer-term indicator of a company's growth. It commonly refers to a company's earnings per share for a particular year.

Ask and bid price: A system used to determine the price a stock can be bought or sold at. A typical purchase may occur at the ask price: the lowest price a seller is willing to accept for a stock. A typical sale may occur at the bid price: the highest price a buyer is willing to pay for a stock. The difference between the two is called the "spread." (*Also, see* Spread)

Asset allocation: The practice of allocating a certain percentage of a portfolio to different types of investments (stocks, bonds, foreign stocks, cash reserves or equivalents, gold, mutual funds, futures, options, etc.).

Averaging up or down in price: After an initial stock purchase, averaging up is the purchase of additional shares of the stock as it moves up in price. Additional purchases might be warranted if the stock is originally purchased at a correct "pivot point" (or buy point) and its price has increased 2% or 3% from the original purchase price. Averaging down is the purchase of additional stock as it declines in price. This is risky. You never know how low a stock could drop. Averaging refers to the combination of prices paid for each purchase of stock divided by the total number of shares purchased. If an initial purchase of 100 shares is made at $50 and a second purchase of 75 shares is made at $51 1/2, the average share price for 175 shares is approximately $50 5/8.

Backlog: A company's total orders or sales received but not yet delivered. (An increase in backlog usually means business is picking up.)

Base (*and* base patterns, base-building, price consolidation area, price pattern): A term used by technical analysts to refer to a stock's chart pattern. It typically can be an indicator for future price advances. This price consolidation generally lasts around seven weeks but can last as long as twelve months. (*Also, see* "Cup with handle," "Double bottom," and "Flat base.")

Bear market: A period when market indices (i.e., Dow Jones Industrial Average, S&P 500, Nasdaq Composite) decline 15% to 25% and in some cases as much as 50%. The trend sometimes lasts about nine months to a year but can be as short as three to six months.

Bid price: (*See* Ask and bid price)

"Big-Cap. Growth Funds vs. Small-Cap. Growth Funds" chart: Found on *Investor's Business Daily*'s "Industry Groups" page. This chart illustrates the degree to which institutions are buying and selling big vs. small-capitalization stocks. This feature helps identify shifts in emphasis by institutions.

Big-cap stock: A stock with a large number of shares outstanding. Microsoft, IBM, and AT&T are considered big-cap stocks.

Blue-chip stock: A nationally known, public company that has a long-standing reputation for quality and good fundamentals, such as earnings and profitability.

Bond: An IOU that represents a loan agreement between the issuer as borrower and the investor as lender. Specified interest is paid periodically, and the principal amount is repaid at final maturity.

Bull market: A period of many months or several years in the overall market cycle where the Dow Jones Industrial Average, S&P 500, and Nasdaq Composite are generally increasing.

Buy point: (*See* "Pivot point")

CAN SLIM: Acronym for William J. O'Neil's investment strategy. CAN SLIM is based on the seven common characteristics found in his study of the greatest stock market winners of the last 45 years. A thorough discussion of CAN SLIM can be found in William J. O'Neil's book, *How to Make Money in Stocks.*

C = Current Earnings Growth

A = Annual Earnings Growth

N = New Products, New Services, New Management, New Price Highs

S = Supply and Demand

L = Leader or Laggard

I = Institutional Sponsorship

M = Market

Cash account: A brokerage account in which all transactions are made in cash. (*Also, see* Margin account)

Channel lines (of a stock, upper and lower): On a stock chart, channel lines are determined by drawing a straight line connecting three of the price peaks and a somewhat parallel line connecting three of the price lows during the same period, usually covering a couple of months. Channel lines drawn over too short a period of time can be premature and incorrect.

"Climax top": When a stock suddenly advances at a much faster rate for one or two weeks after an advance of many months. Generally occurs in the final "stages" of a stock's price advance, indicating a leveling off or decrease in future price movements. Often accompanied by a gap up in price. Based on William J. O'Neil's research, many big market leaders top in this fashion. (*Also, see* Gap *and* Exhaustion gap)

Closed-end funds: Closed-end investment companies have a fixed number of shares to sell. Their shares are traded on the major exchanges and fluctuate according to supply and demand in the market. You do not have a guarantee that you can sell your shares at net asset value as you do in open-end mutual funds.

Commissions (stock, mutual fund, etc.): The fee paid to a broker for purchasing or selling on your behalf.

Commodities: Goods such as agricultural products (soybeans, pork bellies, grains, coffee, etc.), metals, financial indices, wood, and cloth, among others. Sold to investors as commodity futures contracts. (*Also, see* Futures)

Compounding: Generally applied to mutual funds, it involves the continued reinvestment of profits that allows for greater sums of money to work for you over many future years of growth.

Consensus earnings estimate: Combined projections by market analysts of a company's potential earnings for the next year or two.

Contrarian indicators: Specific psychological indicators used by investors who subscribe to contrarian strategies. Historically, when these indicators reach one extreme or another, this foreshadows contrary market activity. For example, some contrarian investors believe that when a large majority of market analysts are bullish, it is likely that the market is about to top. Likewise, when most market analysts are bearish, they believe that the market is preparing for another advance. (*Also, see* Psychological market indicators)

Correction (*or* price correction, pullback, general market correction): A decline in the general market indices or an individual stock.

"Cup with handle": Developed by William J. O'Neil, it is one of three positive chart patterns to look for when doing technical analysis of a stock. It is named such because it resembles the outline of a coffee cup with a handle.

Cyclical stocks/industry groups/sectors: When a stock, industry, or sector moves up or down according to business cycles. (Examples: railroads, airlines, copper, steel, autos, housing, etc.)

Daily Graphs (*and* Daily Graphs Online): Print and online (www.dailygraphs.com) charting services that provide extensive fundamental and technical indicators on thousands of stocks for the individual investor.

Defensive stocks/industry groups/sectors: Usually considered more stable and relatively safer by most investors. They include utilities, tobacco, food, soap, soft drinks, supermarkets, etc. They represent industries of staple goods and repeat purchase items.

Distribution: Selling of stock by large institutions. (*Also, see* Institutional investors)

Diversification: Spreading investment capital over many investments in an attempt to reduce risk in a portfolio. (*Also, see* Asset allocation)

"Double bottom": A William J. O'Neil chart pattern resembling a "W." One of the three positive chart patterns to look for when doing technical analysis of a stock.

Dow Jones Industrial Average (DJIA): Widely followed index that tracks the daily price performance of thirty big-cap, blue-chip companies on the New York Stock Exchange. Generally thought to reflect the overall health of the U.S. economy.

Earnings (*and* earnings growth): Analyzed on both a quarterly and annual basis. Earnings are a basic measurement of a company's ability to make a net profit and grow.

Earnings per share: Calculated by dividing a company's total after-tax profits by the company's number of common shares outstanding. Can be used as an indicator of growth and profitability.

Earnings Per Share (EPS) Rating: Exclusive rating found in *Investor's Business Daily*'s IBD *SmartSelect*™ Corporate Ratings. Stocks are rated on a 1 to 99 scale (with 99 being best) comparing a company's earnings growth on both a current and annual basis with all other publicly traded companies. Stocks with EPS Ratings of 80 or above have outperformed 80% or more of all publicly traded companies in earnings. The EPS Rating combines each company's most recent two quarters of earnings per share growth with its three- to five-year annual growth rate.

Exhaustion gap: A technical term describing that the stock's price opens up on a gap from the prior day's high close. After the stock has had an extended price advance for more than several months. This usually indicates the last stage of a stock's move. (*Also, see* Gap)

Extended (in price): A technical term used to describe the point at which a stock is up in price over its "pivot" or buy point and is considered riskier to buy.

Federal Reserve Board (*or* The Fed): Government agency that monitors, regulates, and exerts influence over the nation's monetary supply, banking system, and interest rates. It often does this by buying or selling government securities and taking other regulatory actions.

Federal Reserve Board's Discount Rate: An important market variable representing what it costs member banks to borrow money from the Fed. A cut in the rate encourages borrowing and increases money supply, whereas a hike in the rate does the opposite.

"52-Week Highs & Lows" feature: Found daily on *Investor's Business Daily*'s "Industry Group" page. Identifies both the top industry sectors with the greatest number of stocks making new price highs as well as lists the individual stocks hitting new highs within that sector ("New Highs" list).

"Flat base": One of three positive chart patterns to look for when doing technical analysis. It usually occurs after a stock has advanced off of a "cup with handle" or "double bottom" pattern. The "flat base" moves straight sideways in a fairly tight price range for at least five weeks and does not correct more than 8% to 12%.

"Follow-through" day: (*See* "1% Follow-through day" concept)

"45-Year Study of the Greatest Stock Market Winners": William J. O'Neil began his investment career as a stockbroker. Over the years, he developed his unique investment strategy by analyzing the greatest stock market winners of all time. This study looked at every piece of fundamental and technical information available on each stock at the time. There were no preconceived notions of certain elements assumed to be important or irrelevant. What William J. O'Neil discovered was that there were seven common characteristics that appeared over and over again, cycle after cycle, from 1953 through today. These common characteristics go by the easy-to-remember acronym CAN SLIM, each letter standing for one of the seven key items. (*Also, see* CAN SLIM)

Fundamental analysis: The numbers and statistics behind each stock. Fundamental analysis evaluates a company's earnings, sales, return on equity, profit margins, balance sheet, share of market, etc. as well as a company's products, management, and industry conditions. Fundamental analysis determines the quality and attractiveness of a stock. (*Also, see* Technical analysis)

Futures trading: A highly speculative and risky endeavor that should not be undertaken without a solid understanding of the marketplace and strong money management techniques. Futures are contracts based on the future delivery of a specific product at a certain time and price. They are generally traded in three product areas: commodity futures, financial futures, and index futures. (*Also, see* Commodities)

Gap (in price): It denotes a day where the stock opens and trades several points above or below the previous day's trading range. It can be identified on a daily chart of a stock's price changes. There are two kinds of gaps: a break away that occurs just after a stock breaks out of a base, and an exhaustion gap that occurs after a stock has advanced for many weeks and is very extended from its most recent base and is close to topping in price. (*Also, see* Exhaustion gap)

General market (*and* general market averages, general market indices): Indices that represent the overall picture of the stock market's health. The most commonly known general market indices are the Dow Jones Industrial Average, the Nasdaq Composite, and the S&P 500.

"General Market & Sectors" page: Found exclusively in *Investor's Business Daily*, this page includes large graphs of each of the major market indices, stacked on top of each other so you can easily identify trends and market divergences. Also included on this page are "The Big Picture," sector charts, and the IBD Mutual Fund Index.

"Groups with the Greatest % of Stocks Making New Highs" list: Found on the "Industry Groups" page of *Investor's Business Daily*, it is a quick way to recognize the top four or five sectors that are the real leaders in the overall market.

Growth fund: A mutual fund that specializes in owning growth stocks. (*Also, see* Growth stocks)

Growth stocks/industry groups/sectors (*and* growth stock investing): Companies, industries, sectors that have a history of rapidly expanding revenues and profits. Growth stocks typically do not pay out dividends. They reinvest this capital into the company for future growth. Three out of four historical big market winners were growth stocks.

Guide to the Markets: (*See* Investor's Business Daily Guide to the Markets)

Handle: Component of William J. O'Neil's "cup with handle" chart pattern. The handle refers to the last segment of the pattern. Handles can be as short as one or two weeks, or a number of weeks longer, and need to drift downward along their lows or have a shakeout. This serves the purpose of getting a needed pullback, or price correction, out of the way. Proper handles rarely pull back in price more than 10% or 15%. They usually show either marked dry-up in volume near their lows, which means there is no more selling of the stock, or they will have several tight areas where the price varies only a tiny amount, and for several weeks may close virtually unchanged in price. (*Also, see* "Cup with handle" *and* Shakeout)

How to Make Money in Stocks: Written by William J. O'Neil, this best-selling investment book (over one million copies sold) illustrates how to buy and sell stocks using the CAN SLIM investment strategy.

Intra-day (or week) high and low price: This represents a day's (or week's) price action in terms of three variables. The top of the bar signifies the highest price the stock traded for the day (or week): this is the intra-day high price. The bottom of the bar marks the low price of the day (or week): this is the intra-day low price. The horizontal intersecting slash shows where the stock closed for the day or (week).

Investor's Business Daily: A time-saving research tool utilizing computerized data to help people make smarter investing decisions. The proprietary information is the result of a comprehensive "45-Year Study of the Greatest Stock Market Winners." *Investor's Business Daily* also provides educational and motivational features to help individuals in their career and personal lives.

Investor's Business Daily Guide to the Markets: Written by the editors of *Investor's Business Daily*, this book provides the background information every investor needs in order to succeed in the market. It explains in detail the various types of investments available today. It also explains how to use fundamental and technical analysis, as well as the features in *Investor's Business Daily*, to make smart investment decisions.

IBD *SmartSelect*™ Corporate Ratings: Five proprietary and exclusive research ratings designed to screen out deficient stocks, identify potential market leaders, save time, and significantly improve stock selection. They include:

Earnings Per Share (EPS) Rating

Relative Price Strength (RS) Rating

Industry Group Relative Strength Rating

Sales+Profit Margins+ROE (SMR) Rating

Accumulation/Distribution Rating

Industry group: Consists of a number of individual companies providing similar services or products. Industries tend to be more specific than sectors.

Industry Group and Ticker Symbol Index: Published by *Investor's Business Daily*, this book lists the stocks in each of *Investor's Business Daily*'s 197 industry groups, sorted three ways (by company name, ticker symbol, and industry group). It can be ordered by calling 800-831-2525.

"Industry Prices" feature: Found each day in *Investor's Business Daily*, it ranks 197 industry groups according to their past six-month price performance, allowing you to easily identify the best and worst performing industries. These 197 industry groups are exclusive to *Investor's Business Daily* and give you a better idea of exactly which industries are the strongest.

Industry Group Relative Strength Rating (*or* Group Strength): *Investor's Business Daily*'s exclusive rating in IBD *SmartSelect*™ Corporate Ratings that compares a stock's industry group price performance over the past six months to the other 196 industry groups (197 total). Graded on an A to E scale, stocks with an A rating are members of the top performing industry groups. E rated stocks belong to the bottom, poorly performing industry groups.

Initial public offering (IPO): The initial offering of shares in a company to the public in order to raise capital for any number of reasons (i.e., reduce debt, research and development, expansion). Shares are sold to investment banks, who then sell them to the public via retail brokerage firms. Research shows that the majority of the best performing stocks began their huge price advances within the first eight years of going public.

Institutional investors: Mutual funds, banks, pension funds, insurance companies, etc., engaged in investing. They are responsible for most of the trading that occurs in the market, and their impact on both an individual stock's price movement as well as the movement of the general market is tremendous.

Institutional sponsorship (*or* Sponsorship): Refers to the shares of a company owned by an institution. The largest sources of demand for stocks are mutual funds and other institutional buyers. It is important to have institutional support behind the stock you're thinking about purchasing. (*Also, see* Institutional investors)

Interest rates: Represents the different prices a bank and other entities charge customers to borrow money.

Leader or laggard: Refers to a company or industry group that is either outperforming or underperforming the general market. To look for top stocks in leading industry groups, refer to the Relative Price Strength Rating and Industry Group Relative Strength Rating in *Investor's Business Daily*.

Management fee (for mutual funds): Small fee, usually half of 1% per year, charged by a mutual fund's management company for supervising and managing the fund's portfolio of stocks.

Management ownership: Percent of common stock which is owned by the company's management; a higher percentage generally assumes an increased level of commitment.

Margin account: A brokerage trading account that allows you to use borrowed money from the brokerage firm when purchasing stocks. (*Also, see* Cash accounts)

Market bottom: Phase that refers to the overall general market making a low point and then turning around for a period of improvement.

"Market Sector Indexes": Small daily industry sector charts in *Investor's Business Daily* located on the "General Market & Sectors" and "Industry Groups" pages. Includes such major sectors as Dow Jones Utilities, High Tech and Defensive. Listed in order of sector relative strength performance. Useful in determining leading sectors in the current market.

Money managers: Professionals that manage portfolios for institutions, i.e., mutual funds, banks, pension funds or insurance companies.

Money market funds: Funds that invest in Treasury bills (T-bills) and the highest grade government obligations.

Mutual fund: A diversified portfolio of stocks managed by a professional investment company for a small management fee. Investors purchase shares in the overall portfolio.

Mutual Fund Index, IBD: Proprietary index of domestic growth stock funds located every day on *Investor's Business Daily*'s "General Market & Sectors" page. Can be used along with other key indices as a general market indicator.

Nasdaq Composite: An index representing the movement of stocks traded by the National Association of Securities Dealers (NASD).

Nasdaq market/exchange: World-wide computer network on which certain stocks are traded "over-the-counter"; unlike the New York Stock Exchange (NYSE) in which stocks are traded on a physical trading floor.

Net asset value: Taking into consideration costs of managing a fund, it is the per-share value of the fund's assets.

New highs: Refers to a stock attaining a new price high when compared to its old price high of the last 52 weeks.

"New Highs" list: (*See* "52-Week Highs & Lows" feature)

New York Stock Exchange (*or* NYSE): Founded in 1792, the oldest and largest exchange in the U.S. where buyers and sellers meet via their brokers to execute buy and sell orders. It is located on Wall Street in New York City.

"1% Follow-Through Day" concept: System developed by William J. O'Neil to identify an important change in general market direction from a definite downtrend to a new uptrend. From the beginning of any attempted rally during a definite downtrend, a "follow-through" day is identified when the index closes up 1% or more for the day on a significant increase in volume from the day before. The first two or three days of a rally are normally disregarded as it has not yet proven it will succeed and "follow-through" with power and conviction. "Follow-through" days therefore generally occur the fourth through seventh day of the attempted rally. They serve as a confirmation that the market has really changed direction and is in a new uptrend.

Options, stock: Purchased contracts to buy (a "call") or sell (a "put") a stock at a specified per-share price by a specified future time period (option expiration date). Options are highly volatile and can involve significant risk.

Paper trading: Tracking "pretend" buys and sells on a piece of paper as a way of getting your feet wet in the market without actually being in the market and trading with real money. Paper trading lacks the emotions of hope and fear one experiences with investing actual money.

"Pivot point" (or buy point): Optimal buy point of a stock as it emerges from a sound and proper basing area or chart pattern (the most common of which include the "cup with handle," "flat base" and "double bottom") and breaks out into a new high in price. This is the point of least resistance and has shown, through William J. O'Neil's research, to have the greatest chance of moving substantially higher based on its current and historical price and volume activity.

Portfolio management: Refers to how many stocks you own and the important weighting, strategies and methods used to add to, reduce or sell stocks; how you change your mix and make decisions as time goes by.

Post-analysis: Vital process of evaluating your successes and mistakes in the stock market by posting all previous buys and sells on charts for a specified time frame and separating out those that made money from those that were losses. Allows investors a way to improve their future performance by realistically learning from past decisions.

Price/earnings (P/E) ratio: Theoretically measures the value of a stock by dividing the current price by its earnings per share over the last twelve months. When a stock's P/E ratio is high, it is considered by the majority of investors as pricey or overvalued. Stocks with low P/Es are typically considered a good value. However, through his studies of the biggest stock market winners, William J. O'Neil found the opposite to be true: the higher the P/E, the better the stock. The average P/E of the best winners over the last fifteen years at the initial buy point *prior* to their huge price increases was 31 times earnings. These P/Es went on to expand more than 100% to over 70 times earnings as the stocks significantly increased in price. P/Es are misunderstood and misused by many investors.

Price-to-book value: Compares a stock's value in the market (determined by the current stock price) to the value of total company assets less total company liabilities (book value). Based on the "45-Year Study of the Greatest Stock Market Winners," this measurement did not prove to be significant among winning stocks.

Price and volume chart: Daily, weekly or monthly basis graphs that show a stock's price and volume history. Used by most professional investors today to assist in the timing and selection of stocks.

Price consolidation area: (*See* Base)

Price line/price plot on a chart: The horizontal line on a chart represents a stock's price history. Each thin vertical line represents a day's (or week's) price action, indicating the highest and lowest price the stock traded for that day or week. The small intersecting horizontal slash shows where the stock closed for that same time period.

Price pattern: (*See* Base)

Prior uptrend: Phrase used by chart readers to denote the trend of price movement over several months immediately preceding a stock's chart base-building period. Healthy stocks show a prior uptrend where the stock outperforms the general market. Laggards or poor stocks display a prior downtrend.

Profit and loss statement: A corporate quarterly or annual report that shows a firm's profitability, identifying both income and expenses.

Profit margins (pre-tax, after-tax): Measure of a company's profitability calculated by dividing annual earnings by revenues, displayed as a percentage. A higher and improving profit margin indicates a more profitable company. Can be calculated by dividing either a company's pre-tax earnings (pre-tax profit margins) or after-tax earnings (after-tax profit margins) by revenues.

Prospectus: Formal lengthy printed statement released by a company or mutual fund and is required by the Securities and Exchange Commission (SEC). It includes a company's or fund's business or investing strategy/objective, plan, short and long-term performance figures, risk, competition, holdings, management information, etc.

Psychological market indicators: Various technical measurements such as "ratio of put volume to call volume," "% of market advisors bullish vs. bearish" etc., that attempt to measure the psychology of investors.

Put-call ratio: The trading volume of put (sell) options divided by the volume of call (buy) options in the marketplace. A high ratio (more puts than calls) is a sign of excessive bearishness or negativity in the market and has historically indicated the opposite, i.e., that the market may be headed for an upturn or a bullish phase.

Rally (*and* false rally): An attempt by a stock or the general market to turn and advance in price after a period of decline. Successful rallies are usually identified by more consistent price increases on greater than normal volume. False rallies are generally signified by increases in price but a lack of big or increased volume, indicating absence of large buying in the market. False rallies frequently either do not last as long or do not recover as much in price.

Relative strength line: Available in most good charting services, relative strength line compares a stock's price performance versus the overall market. If a relative strength line in trending up, the stock is outperforming the broader market (S&P 500). If it is trending downward, it is lagging the general market. It is normally wise to avoid stocks showing an overall downtrend in their relative strength lines.

Relative Price Strength (RS) Rating (*or relative strength*): Exclusive rating in *Investor's Business Daily*. This IBD *SmartSelect*™ Corporate Rating measures each stock's price performance over the latest twelve months compared to all other stocks. Stocks rating below 70 indicate weaker or more laggard relative price performance.

Return on equity (ROE): An indicator of a company's financial performance. It measures how efficient a company is with its money. The biggest stock market winners historically showed an ROE of 17% to 50% before they made their huge gains.

Sales growth: A company's annual and quarterly rate of increase in revenues (sales). A measure of growth and success as long as it is accompanied by an equally strong rate of increase in earnings per share. You want to see both in a potential investment.

Sales+Profit Margins+ROE (SMR) Rating: Unique measurement pioneered by *Investor's Business Daily* to help investors identify companies that show superior sales growth, profit margins and return on equity when compared to all other stocks. Rated on a scale from A to E, with A = the top 20% in terms of sales, margins and ROE; B = the top 40%, etc. This is one of the five IBD *SmartSelect*™ Corporate Ratings.

Sectors: Consist of a number of similar industry groups. Sectors are broader than industries. For instance, the high-tech or consumer sector can include several different industries.

Sector charts: Found on the "General Markets & Sectors" page of *Investor's Business Daily*, these charts show the last three months' percentage increases for the leading sectors. Sector charts are useful in determining the strength of each sector.

Securities & Exchange Commission (SEC): A government "watch-dog" agency created to regulate and monitor the securities industry.

Shakeout: A sharp pullback or correction in the price of a stock (generally below a recent low point) that scares people out, and then turns around and advances.

Short sellers (*or selling short*): Investors that borrow shares of a stock from their brokerage firm and then sell the shares of the stock hoping it will go down in price. They must later purchase the borrowed shares on the open market (presumably for less than they sold it for previously), making money between the initial sale and the subsequent buy back at a lower price. Short selling is difficult and not recommended for new or inexperienced investors.

Small-cap stocks: Companies that have a relatively small number of shares of common stock outstanding.

SmartSelect™: (*See* IBD *SmartSelect™* Corporate Ratings)

Sponsorship: (*See* Institutional sponsorship)

Sponsorship Rating: Unique *Investor's Business Daily* rating that helps investors know if a company's stock is owned by the better performing mutual funds and if more mutual funds have bought the stock recently. Rated on a scale from A to E, with A = indicating the top 20% of better performing funds and increased ownership, B = the top 40%, etc.

Spread, market makers (*or price spread*): The gap between the bid (the price at which an investor can sell shares of a stock) and the ask (or offer price) of a stock. All stocks on the NYSE and Nasdaq have varying spreads between their bid and ask.

"Stage" of base: A term referring to the number or "stage" of the bases a stock will form as it advances on its way up in price. Successful stock advances over a year can consist of two, three or four bases on the way up before going into a major decline. The initial base is referred to as a "first stage" base, the second base as the "second stage," etc.

Stalling of price (on one of the indices): A term indicating a type of price activity occurring on one of the market indices (the Dow, S&P 500 or Nasdaq Composite). It occurs when the index price closes barely up, unchanged or slightly down on increased volume from the day before after having advanced noticeably for several days. This indicates distribution or selling in the index at that point.

Standard & Poor's 500 (S&P 500): An index of 500 major companies. The breakdown: 400 industrial firms, 20 transportation firms, 40 utilities, and 40 financial firms. This index is market value weighted.

Technical analysis: Study of a stock or general market's price and volume movement, mainly by use of charts to analyze buying and selling in the market.

10Ks/10Qs: A 10K is an annual corporate report required by the SEC; 10Qs are required quarterly reports. They provide a comprehensive overview of a company's recent state of business.

36-Month Mutual Fund Performance Rating: Exclusive letter rating (A+ to E) that tracks the three-year total return performance record of every mutual fund. Funds with an A+ rating are in the top 5% in terms of performance. Funds with an A rating are in the top 10%, and so on.

Turnaround stock: Company that has been doing poorly for some time but is now turning its sales and earnings back up, usually due to new management, new products or a major improvement in industry conditions. Historically, only one in four past big winners began from a turnaround situation.

Turnover rate: The number of shares traded per year as a percentage of shares held by a mutual fund. An indicator of a fund's trading activity. Many aggressive growth funds have higher turnover rates.

Value investing: An investing strategy that focuses on companies believed to be undervalued (indicated by low price-to-earnings [P/E] ratios, low price-to-book value, etc.). Value stocks are typically viewed as being bargain-priced and a good value. This strategy focuses on fundamentals and less on technicals. A value fund is a mutual fund that invests in undervalued stocks.

Volatility: A measure of the degree of fluctuation in a stock's price. Volatility is exemplified by large, frequent price swings up and down.

Volume: Number of shares a stock trades either per day or per week. One of the important keys to interpreting supply and demand for a stock.

Volume Percent Change: Exclusive measurement in *Investor's Business Daily* that alerts you to unusual trading in a stock. This measurement tracks the average daily volume of a stock over the past fifty trading days and shows you how much above or below average the stock traded yesterday. It helps you track the flow of institutional money in and out of stocks.

Wedging: Technical term referring to how the handle area of a "cup with handle" price pattern moves up over a period of a week, just prior to the "pivot," or buy point. This is not a constructive signal. Proper handles should show a drifting off or a minor downtrend prior to the breakout point. Handles that wedge up tend to indicate a faulty pattern and are prone to failure.

"Where the Big Money's Flowing" list: Important daily list in *Investor's Business Daily* that highlights stocks that had the greatest percentage increase in volume above their normal past daily trading level. Usually a sign that institutions are buying or selling stock. Found at the beginning of both the NYSE and Nasdaq stock tables.

William O'Neil + Co., Incorporated: Institutional research firm established in 1963 that created the first daily U.S. equity database based on models of the greatest stock market winners since 1953. Today it provides computerized stock research to over 400 of the largest worldwide institutional investors. Sister company to *Investor's Business Daily*.

Index

About the Author

William J. O'Neil is the founder and chairman of *Investor's Business Daily* and the author of the million-copy best-seller *How to Make Money in Stocks*. Born in Oklahoma and raised in Texas, William J. O'Neil began his investment career as a stockbroker. He started investing with less than $500, but through continued study, mistakes, and a desire to find out exactly how the stock market *really* worked, O'Neil realized a 20-fold increase in his own account in the 26 months from October 1962 to December 1964. He then purchased a seat on the New York Stock Exchange and opened his own investment management and research firm, William O'Neil + Co., Incorporated, at the age of 30.

Founded in 1963, William O'Neil + Co. was the first to create a computerized stock-market database, which is used today by over 400 major U.S. institutions across the country, including banks, insurance companies, pension and mutual funds, corporations, and government organizations. O'Neil wanted to provide individuals with the same critical data the professionals use in order to make smarter investment decisions, so he launched *Investor's Business Daily* in 1984. By virtue of a proprietary contract with William O'Neil + Co., *Investor's Business Daily* is able to access the historical securities database for use in publication of the newspaper.

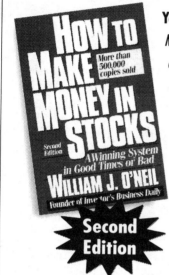